The Nevada Review

Caleb S. Cage
Editor-in-Chief

Joe McCoy
Managing Editor

Volume 1   Fall 2009   Number 1

Contents

3   Editorial Essay
Caleb S. Cage & Joe McCoy

5   William J. Raggio: The Consummate Prosecutor
Michael Archer

14   Harder Than Folsom: Johnny Cash, Reno, and the Fourth Wall
Caleb S. Cage

27   The Politics of Higher Education:
Why the Nevada Board of Regents Should Be Appointed
Jeremy McKay

52   Fiction: "9/10"
Brad Summerhill

65   Interview: **Dr. Gary Cage**, Foothills Church of Christ

89   Book Reviews
Literary Nevada: Writings from the Silver State.
Cheryll Glotfelty. (Reno: University of Nevada Press, 2008)
Reviewed by **Alisha Anne Sullivan**

91 *Reno's Big Gamble: Image and Reputation in the Biggest Little City.*
Alicia Barber. (Lawrence: University Press of Kansas, 2008)
Reviewed by **Caleb S. Cage**

94 *Nevada Ghost Towns and Mining Camps.*
Stanley W. Paher. (Berkley, CA: Howell North, 1970)
Reviewed by **Lee Johnson**

Cover art photography by **Larry Neel** entitled "Storm Over Big Smoky Valley." Mr. Neel specializes in wildlife photography, and his work has featured a variety of themes including landscape, historic buildings, and portraits. His work can be viewed at larryneelphoto.photium.com.

The Nevada Review is a journal dedicated to Nevada: it aims to enhance understanding of the state as a geographical, social, and political unit and a microcosm of the West in the broader historical and political development of the United States. Recognizing the distinctive geological, environmental, social and ethnographic characteristics of Nevada, the *Review* seeks contributions that examine these features and investigate how they have contributed to the shape of its political institutions, demographic profile, and cultural mores. To this end, the *Review* encompasses studies from a broad range of disciplines and perspectives, including, but not limited to, history, political science, economics, and literary criticism and also accepts literary contributions of short fiction that concern Nevada, its people, and their way of life.

The Nevada Review is published biannually in the fall and spring. Contributions to each issue of *The Nevada Review* will be obtained both through solicitation by the editors as well as through unsolicited submissions. The editors do not stipulate that all unsolicited articles will receive responses. Authors may send their work to *The Nevada Review* · P.O. Box 1582 · Reno, NV 89505, and submissions should be typed, double-spaced, and sent in duplicate along with a copy on disk in IBM© compatible form (Word Perfect© 5.1 or 6.0 or Microsoft Word©). Authors should consult the most recent edition of the University of Chicago Press *Manual of Style*. All noted material should be in the form of endnotes and should appear consecutively, double-spaced, and as part of the body of the text. Correspondence concerning articles and essays is welcomed and should be directed in the form of a written letter to the editor. © *The Nevada Review*, 2009.

Editorial Essay
CALEB S. CAGE & JOE MCCOY

It is no exaggeration to say that *The Nevada Review*, like the contributions found within its pages, was born from a love of and fascination with the state of Nevada, its geographical beauty, its unique history as well as its cultural and demographic peculiarities. It is the hope of the editors that the *Review* will find a readership that shares these sensibilities and wishes to learn more about this land, its people, and its stories.

In launching *The Nevada Review*, we aim to provide a forum for those interested in reading and writing about any and all matters related to this State. We propose a type of journal where the subject of Nevada can be examined from within and from without, that is, from as many perspectives as there are persons drawn to this central theme. We believe that such a forum can play a small though significant role in enhancing understanding of Nevada by investigating the shape of its political institutions, demographic profile, and cultural mores.

To this end, the present volume and each subsequent edition of *The Nevada Review* will seek to encompass studies from a broad range of disciplines and perspectives, including, but not limited to, history, political science, economics, and literary criticism, and will also include literary contributions of short fiction that concern Nevada, its people, and their way of life.

Producing a high quality journal that attracts both an academic and policy-minded readership as well as a general interest audience is one of the driving forces behind the production of *The Nevada Review*. It is the editors' first priority to ensure that each publication presents the finest research and reflections on Nevada by the highest caliber scholars, writers, and thinkers that the State has to offer.

We believe that the present volume is representative of the comprehensive and eclectic array of contributions that future issues will feature. In this our inaugural issue, the reader will find a excerpt from the life of State Senator William J. Raggio, authored by Michael Archer, recounting an episode drawn from his time as Washoe County District Attorney; Caleb S. Cage's historical exploration of what is perhaps the most famous line Johnny Cash ever wrote: "I shot a man in Reno just to watch him die"; and Jeremy McKay's institutional history and analysis of the Nevada Board of Regents. In addition, the *Review* is very fortunate to be able to present Brad Summerhill's fiction piece entitled "9/10" as well as an interview with Dr. Gary T. Cage, a Reno minister who has been serving his congregation for 30 years. Also Larry Neel's photograph, "Storm Over Big Smoky Valley," not only represents a perfect Nevada scene, but is also a wonderful artistic piece for the cover of this volume. We would also like to acknowledge in sincere gratitude the work of Alisha Anne Sullivan and Lee Johnson in composing their respective book reviews. The editors would also like to thank Alisha Anne Sullivan and Sharon Wurm for graciously assisting with the editing of this first issue.

We hope that you will enjoy these contributions and that you will choose to make *The Nevada Review* a part of your regular reading in the future. ∎

William J. Raggio: The Consummate Prosecutor
Michael Archer

Throughout his long and distinguished legislative career, Nevada State Senator William J. Raggio has been admired for his intellect, eloquence, and a statesmanship that allows him to focus on the most important facets of any issue and invariably to forge agreement on what is best for the State. Political observers attribute the Senator's great success to his talent for presenting his point of view in a methodical, reasoned, and persuasive manner, often extemporaneously on the floor of the Nevada Senate. What has sometimes been forgotten is that Bill Raggio honed these skills to a surgical edge during nearly 19 years as a prosecuting attorney for Washoe County.

His legendary career as District Attorney began in 1959 with a series of challenges so intense and risky that they might have broken a person of lesser character and resolve. During just his first 18 months in office, the 39-year-old D.A. disrupted the corrupting influence of the local underworld by sending Joe Conforte to prison for extortion, after the notorious pimp attempted to ensnare Bill in a tryst with an underage girl. This precipitated the colorful event for which Raggio would be most remembered over the years in the minds of the public: burning down a Conforte brothel near Wadsworth, Nevada.

At the same time, Bill was engaged in a dangerous battle, both personally and politically, to rid the Reno Police Department and City Council of rampant corruption. As if this whirlwind of activity were not enough, the D.A. also found himself personally prosecuting several cold-blooded murderers.

By the end of his first term, Raggio would successfully accomplish all these goals and earn additional notoriety for bringing about the swift conviction of Thomas Lee Bean for the murder, rape, and ghastly dismemberment of British Olympic skier, Sonja McCaskie.

Previous works of Reno-based author, Michael Archer, include a book entitled, *A Patch of Ground: Khe-Sahn Remembered*. The following essay contains excerpts from his forthcoming book about the life of William J. Raggio, which is scheduled for release in early 2010 by Hellgate Press, Ashland, OR.

Highly regarded by his peers, Bill was honored by the National District Attorney's Association as being the "Outstanding Prosecutor in the United States for 1964." Such distinction was rare for a "small town" D.A. Three years later, Raggio would be elected president of that prestigious organization.

In the midst of this hectic period, Bill was called upon to prosecute Robert "Sandman" Williams, who had committed a double-homicide in a Washoe County courtroom—just 20 feet from the District Attorney's office door. Williams would later plead not guilty by reason of insanity. District Attorney Raggio did not deny that the Sandman was mentally ill. Yet, because Raggio understood the gradations of that defense better than most attorneys in the country, he knew it did not necessarily mean Williams should not be held accountable for the crime.

The defense counsel for Robert Williams was another legal legend, southern Nevada's Harry E. Claiborne. Though merciless competitors within the courtroom, Bill and Harry were good friends and great admirers of the other's ability.

Flamboyant, hard drinking, and with an eye for attractive women, Claiborne epitomized the aura of 1960's Las Vegas. He regularly associated with the famous and the infamous. Yet he could also achieve extraordinary rapport with the average person, particularly jury members, who loved his charm, quick wit, and talent for storytelling. As former Clark County District Attorney George Dickerson later described him, "Harry Claiborne was without a doubt the greatest criminal defense lawyer in the southwest United States."

On Thanksgiving Eve, November 23, 1960, just a few months after conclusion of the sensational Joe Conforte and Thayne Archibald trials, the relative tranquility of the Washoe County Courthouse was rocked again—this time by gunshots.

A contentious civil case had gone badly and 52-year old Robert Williams pulled a .38 caliber, automatic pistol from his jacket and shot opposing counsel. Williams, known locally as the "Sandman," owned a small gravel pit on West Fourth Street in Reno, which he operated alone by using an antiquated machine to load sand and gravel onto his old truck for delivery around town. The Sandman also lived at the gravel pit in a shanty with no indoor plumbing. Reclusive and unwashed, he frequently exhibited erratic, often explosive, behavior and was known to the District Attorney's Office as "an agitator."

His estranged wife, Joyce, and her mother, were each asking for a one-third interest in the gravel pit business. Robert Williams disagreed, and the civil proceeding on November 23rd was intended to adjudicate the matter.

Robert had already received a continuance in the case alleging, through his attorney Sam Francovich, that he was hospitalized for a heart condition. Judge Jon Collins ordered the bailiff go to Washoe Medical Center to check the veracity of this claim. Williams was indeed an inpatient at the time. Anxious to settle this case so he could return to Ely to meet his judicial responsibilities there, Judge Collins ordered Williams to be in court the following day.

Robert appeared as scheduled; however, toward the end of the court proceeding, he claimed to be experiencing severe chest pains and went into the hallway. Francovich asked the judge for a continuance until after Thanksgiving. The judge denied it saying, "We are going to finish this case today," and ordered Robert back into the small, temporary courtroom that was being used to hear the case.

The Sandman returned and minutes later opened fire on opposing counsel. Before Sam Francovich could wrestle the gun from Williams, Eli Liverato, a 34-year-old father of three children, was dead. Edwin Mulcahy was seriously wounded, as was a third victim, G. Waldron Snyder, an Ohio lawyer and brother of one of the litigants in the case.

Questioned immediately after the shooting, Williams claimed to have no memory of the event. District Attorney Raggio, who had run to the scene of the shooting from his nearby office, soon issued a complaint charging Robert Williams with the murder of Liverato. "This was a tragic thing," Bill later told the press. "The whole community has been shocked by it."

Edwin Mulcahy, a long-time assistant district attorney for Washoe County, had been in court that day as a private attorney—still an accepted practice for lawyers working in the District Attorney's Office in order to supplement their incomes. He and Bill Raggio had been friends since Bill's early days as an assistant district attorney.

Raggio regularly visited his wounded friend in the intensive care unit of Washoe Medical Center. Several days after the shooting, as Bill was about to leave the hospital room, Ed whispered to him, "Let's get this guy [Williams]." "I will," Bill promised solemnly. Mulcahy died a few hours later.

Because of the public outrage against Robert Williams for the murder of these two popular family men, special arrangements were made to incarcerate him at the Nevada State Prison in Carson City while awaiting trial. It was also difficult to find a local attorney who would represent Williams. At last, attorney Harry Claiborne of Las Vegas agreed to take the case *pro bono*.

In his 2004 oral history, Claiborne would recall being contacted by Nevada Supreme Court Justice Milton Badt who was "very upset" that Robert Williams had been unable to obtain adequate defense counsel. Within two days of the shooting, all major law firms in Reno had filed a suit bearing the names of 23 lawyers as plaintiffs in civil cases against Williams, thus precluding them from being appointed to act in his defense. Sam Francovich, the Sandman's attorney of record, was excluded because he would be called as a witness.

Claiborne told Judge Badt, "I will defend him, but if there is that much prejudice, I suggest they bring in a visiting judge from somewhere." As it turned out, Judge Merwyn Brown of Winnemucca was brought in to hear the case. Due to previous contacts that had not gone well, neither Harry nor Judge Brown, were great admirers of the other. "I was flabbergasted when Judge Brown was appointed," Claiborne later stated. "He was not a very knowledgeable judge … and knew less about the rules of evidence than probably any judge in the State. I was constantly frustrated by his rulings."

Harry Claiborne would later say that the Robert Williams' case was the most difficult he ever tried, largely because Bill Raggio chose to handle the prosecution personally. "There's [been] no better prosecutor—ever—in the State than Bill Raggio."

The trial of Robert "Sandman" Williams began June 28, 1961. There was initially some difficulty seating jurors due to the prejudicial nature of crime. Eventually, eleven men and one woman were empanelled.

The case hinged upon a determination of Williams' mental state at the time of the shooting. To help clarify this complex issue, most courts at the time relied on the "McNaughton Rule," a common law principle established 120 years earlier by British jurists which held that a criminal act was not excused if the defendant knew the nature and quality of the act *and* knew that it was wrong. Bill Raggio had a good deal of experience prosecuting cases in which the so-called "insanity defense" was argued. The most notable case was that of Robert Fox who had murdered his wife and then unsuccessfully attempted to take his own life.

As Raggio would later recall:

> The Fox case was one of the principal experiences of my trial attorney career, and I learned a lot, not only from what we did, but from what the defense put forth. Because of it, I became conversant with the parlance, terminology, and workings of psychiatrists and the evaluations that they utilized in these kinds of cases. We had several psychiatrists on both sides of the case. One psychiatrist was Dr. Rudolph Toller, the Director of the State Psychiatric Hospital in Stockton, California. He was a brilliant guy and very good witness who I would use often through my career.
>
> I really enjoyed cross-examining psychiatrists. The McNaughton Rule allowed me a trial tactic where I would get the defense's expert witnesses so far out on a limb with what they were saying, they could no longer defend their position. The testimony would ultimately fall apart when I asked one final question: "Would this defendant have committed the act if there had been a police officer standing there?" If the answer was "no," then the defendant did know the nature and quality of his action, and that it was wrong. The psychiatrist would then usually pronounce a diagnosis. I'd then pick up a copy of the *Diagnostic and Statistical Manual of Mental Disorders* and read each element of the diagnosis to see if they all applied. They almost never did. As I said, I loved cross-examining psychiatrists.

The effectiveness of this tactic was borne out a few days later when Robert Fox was found guilty of first-degree murder and sentenced to death. For years thereafter, *State v. Fox* would be cited in legal proceedings across the country as a significant precedent in criminal cases involving the insanity defense.

By the time Sandman Williams went to trial, Bill Raggio understood the McNaughton standard better than almost every prosecuting attorney in the country. Despite his recent promise to a dying friend, Bill's zealous prosecution of this case was not the result of *vendetta*; it was, rather, his unwavering belief that Williams had premeditated his act and had known "right from wrong" when he was pulling the trigger. As such, the most important testimony would be that of the psychiatrists.

Defense attorney Claiborne, though not being paid for defending Williams, did petition Judge Brown for funds to hire a psychiatrist. Brown offered to appoint a local one. "I don't want a local psychiatrist," Harry replied. "There's too damn much prejudice. I want somebody who is well-known and well-respected, and frankly I don't believe any of the doctors you mentioned [from the Reno area] are really qualified anyway." Judge Brown denied his request for funds.

Claiborne used $600 of his own money to hire Dr. Raymond Schmidt, who had acquired a reputation for his work at San Quentin Prison. Dr. Schmidt came to the Washoe County Jail, where Williams had been moved from the State prison as his trial date neared, and examined him for a day and a half. Schmidt came away convinced that Robert Williams was legally insane and would become Claiborne's main defense witness at the trial.

Dr. Schmidt testified for nearly an entire day, repeatedly stating that, in his opinion, Robert Williams was too insane to have understood what he was doing at the time of the murders. Schmidt, said Williams, had not intended to kill anyone when he went to court that day, but became "absolutely powerless" to stop himself at the time of the shooting.

The prosecution called Dr. Rudolph Toller and then Dr. Richard Brown to the stand. Raggio had selected Dr. Brown as a prosecution expert because he was a "reasonable, centrist psychiatrist."

Harry Claiborne hammered away at the doctor's testimony seeking to define the point where Williams might have switched from legal sanity to insanity. At one point, Claiborne was able to get Dr. Brown to admit that Williams might not have had any control of himself after he fired the first shot. This, in some ways, paralleled Dr. Schmidt's earlier testimony, the key issue being whether Williams knew right from wrong when he fired the *first* shot.

On redirect examination by District Attorney Raggio, Dr. Brown testified that Williams did know right from wrong throughout the entire episode, though he may not have had total control over his actions. Dr. Brown stated that Robert Williams had no recollection of the shooting incident. Further, when Williams was told within moments of the shooting that he had killed Liverato, he showed no reaction.

Dr. Brown's analysis came from a transcript of the November 23, 1960, property partition trial and from a subsequent interview with Williams just minutes after the shooting. Brown termed Williams' mental illness to be "a paranoid personality with manic depression." The psychiatrist went on to describe Williams as a methodical man until his marriage began falling apart three years before. At that point, Williams found his methods no longer worked for him, and he began blaming others for his failings.

Sharp exchanges between Raggio and Claiborne punctuated the trial, with Claiborne derisively referring to the District Attorney as "Dr. Raggio."

When Judge Jon Collins was called to testify, he became the target of Claiborne's most ruthless personal attack. Harry first pointed out that Judge Collins had brought his own court reporter with him from Ely to help work his cases in Reno the previous November. The defense attorney then described in detail the account given by witnesses who said Collins had ducked down behind the bench to avoid being shot and then crawled out of the room on his hands and knees—"leaving his staff in the courtroom." The implication was that the judge had acted in a cowardly manner during the shooting, though it had nothing to do with Williams' culpability for the crime.

Bill Raggio was familiar with Claiborne's often-vicious courtroom tactics. According to him:

> That was Harry Claiborne's style, especially if he didn't have the facts of the case working in his favor. He would "take off" on a witness. Harry believed in histrionics, a lot of courtroom drama. He recognized that many jurors liked his loud and demonstrative manner, particularly his antagonism of judges. Harry would purposely provoke a judge in front of a jury in order to have the judge rebuke him, thus garnering sympathy from some of the jurors. I liken it to a basketball coach intentionally drawing a technical foul in order to stir up the crowd.

Harry decided to put the babbling and irrational Williams on the witness stand to demonstrate his insanity to the jury. D.A. Raggio wisely chose not to pursue a withering cross-examination. Claiborne would recall:

> Bill Raggio did not try to do much with him [i.e. Williams]. He knew if he fooled around with him too long it was going to increase the damage to his case. Bill was not only the best prosecutor I ever worked with but also one of the most clever. He was the ultimate. I've tried murder cases in 15 different states. Nobody could carry his briefcase.

On the afternoon of July 11, 1961, Judge Brown instructed the jury on six possible verdicts they could entertain, ranging from first- and second-degree murder to not guilty or not guilty by reason of insanity. They then began deliberating the fate of Robert "Sandman" Williams.

Just prior to that, in his final argument, District Attorney William Raggio had asked the jury to send Williams to the gas chamber for "the most cold-blooded, brutal slaying in the State's history." Bill told the jury that Williams had "convenient amnesia" in forgetting the shooting and accused defense attorney Harry Claiborne of throwing up "a smokescreen to protect his client." Alluding to Claiborne's "style," Raggio told jurors that Harry had "tried everyone in the courtroom *except* Robert Williams."

"Mr. Raggio wants to kill my client," Claiborne declared in closing. He asked the jury to believe Dr. Schmidt, the San Quentin prison psychiatrist, who said Williams had been insane for years and should have been committed. He urged them to believe that Dr. Schmidt was more credible because he "had no interest in the case" unlike Dr. Rudolph Toller, whom he labeled "a prosecution specialist." Bill Raggio would later remark:

> I selected psychiatric experts for the prosecution who I thought would sound the most reasonable to the jury. Of course, we always ran up against the issue that the doctors were paid by the District Attorney's Office when they testified as expert witnesses for the prosecution. But since the defense side did exactly the same thing, I don't think that accusation had much of an impact on jurors.

The following day, the jury returned a verdict of first-degree murder. Three days later, Judge Merwyn Brown sentenced Robert Williams to life imprisonment. In contrast to his stoic demeanor throughout the trial, Williams required help getting to his feet to hear the sentence and broke into uncontrollable sobbing as it was being read.

When asked later how he felt about not getting the death penalty he sought, Bill Raggio replied, "I was not surprised because I sensed a certain level of sympathy within the jury." Harry Claiborne's take on the verdict was more in keeping with his flair for the dramatic: "If there was ever a son-of-a-bitch ticketed for the electric chair, it was him [i.e. Williams]. I felt I saved his life, and of course, I did."

Claiborne's remark underscores the effectiveness of Bill Raggio as a prosecutor. It was rare when he did not get the sentence he sought, particularly in a capital case. Because of the foresight and attention to detail he put into preparation for every case, it was even more uncommon to have the verdict successfully appealed.

Robert "Sandman" Williams would die of natural causes while serving his sentence in the Nevada State Prison.

Harry Claiborne's unorthodox and antagonistic style, upon which his legend was built, also proved to be his Achilles' heel. This was particularly true of his undisguised contempt for the intrusiveness of the federal strike force in Las Vegas, a unit he once publicly referred to as "a bunch of crooks."

In 1978, Claiborne was appointed federal judge for the United States District Court for the District of Nevada, and his subsequent rulings, often in favor of those being prosecuted by the strike force, raised the ire of federal law enforcement. A concerted effort was made to remove him from the bench.

In December 1983, Judge Claiborne was indicted by a federal grand jury for bribery, fraud, and tax evasion. Much of the federal case hinged upon the testimony of Joe Conforte, a former client of Claiborne's. After federal prosecutors successfully petitioned for a change of venue to Reno, Bill Raggio, then in private practice, leapt at the opportunity to join with attorney Oscar Goodman in defending his friend, Judge Claiborne, against his old nemesis, Conforte.

Bill was familiar with Conforte's predilection for compulsive lying and so thoroughly destroyed his credibility on the witness stand that federal prosecutors were forced to drop the bribery and fraud charges. Judge Claiborne was convicted three months later of income tax evasion. He would serve 17 months in prison, during which time he was impeached by the U.S. House of Representatives, tried by the Senate, and removed from the federal bench. He died in January 2004. ■

Harder Than Folsom:
Johnny Cash, Reno, and the Fourth Wall
Caleb S. Cage

In 1873, Nevada Governor Lewis "Broadhorns" Bradley addressed the Legislature, suggesting that the State Prison be moved from Warm Springs near Carson City to Reno, as John M. Townely recounts in his definitive history of Reno from 1868 to 1900, *Tough Little Town on the Truckee*. It was a cost-saving exercise for Bradley: The inmates could build the prison, pay their own way by using the waterpower of the Truckee River to turn out industrial goods, and the old prison in Warm Springs could be used as the State's asylum. With an interested partner in the city of Reno and a friendly Democrat-led Legislature, Bradley promised to choose the location for the new prison in Reno by June of that year.

By 1874, the location for the new facility had been chosen, and $100,000 had been allocated for its construction. As Townley describes it, the prison "was to measure 450' x 500' with foundations nine feet deep and seven wide, topped with twenty-six foot high walls, five feet thick at the base and three feet at the peak." Security was planned in as well, with "towers at each corner that would be connected with walkways." By November, the job had been contracted, and the site was being surveyed and excavated, only to be shut down for the winter months around Thanksgiving.

1875 would prove to be the year that the plan started falling apart. The Legislature had flipped into Republican control, and the controlling party was eager to stall Bradley's boon to the growing city of Reno. Studying the finances of the prison, they found that money was being misspent, and so they refused to allocate the additional $300,000 that the contractor would need to finish the job. Due to the money constraints on the project, the contractor received a new contract to finish construction on all but the northern wall of the facility, with the

---

Caleb S. Cage is the co-author of *The Gods of Diyala: Transfer of Command in Iraq*, which documents his experiences as a U.S. Army officer in Iraq. He is currently serving as a Senior Policy Advisor to Nevada Lt. Governor Brian Krolicki, and he is working on two books on the life and music of Johnny Cash.

assumption that the political battle would subside in time for the final financial provisions for the fourth wall.

By the 1877 Legislative Session, everything seemed to favor finalizing the move of the prison to Reno. Unfortunately for those in Reno who wished to bring the state dollars into their city, private politics nixed the deal when C. C. Powning, the owner and editor of Reno's newspaper, *The Nevada State Journal*, decided to punish his political enemies by opposing the deal. By the end of the session, the issue was dead, and the three walls of the prison crumbled after being used as a skating rink in the winter and a cattle stable in the summer by the local populace.

Johnny Cash might have found this story amusing when he took the stage at the Nevada State Prison near Carson on July 30, 1973, one hundred years after Bradley embarked upon his mission to relocate the prison. If the prison move had succeeded, Cash might have enjoyed the raucous applause of Reno's inmates when he sang to them that he had once "shot a man in Reno just to watch him die." He might have appreciated the opportunity to celebrate his near fifty prison performances, a Christian obligation as he told the *Nevada State Journal*, with the Reno inmates as well.

Cash would have also appreciated the symbolism of the missing fourth wall of the prison, especially a prison in Reno, because of the themes of prison and life outside the boundaries of the law and respectable society—so prevalent in country and folk music—that he raised to the level of high art, most notably with his "Reno line." Responding to a question about the origins of his famous "Reno line" in an interview with Steve Pond of *Rolling Stone* magazine in December of 1992, Cash quickly dispensed with the Reno question: "No," Cash said, [the "Reno line"] was from my head. It was from a violent movie, and I just wanted to write a song that would tell what I thought it would be like to be in prison." Just as quickly, he moved the conversation towards his appreciation for the confined lives of the prisoners: "Merle Haggard came up with a great line after I had those prison hits and after he got out of prison. He said, 'Johnny Cash understands what it's like to be in prison, but he doesn't know.'"

Cash understood what it was like to be in prison because he had spent his lifetime being trapped between contradicting themes and pursuits. In his second autobiography, *Cash,* he endorses a line about himself by his friend Kris Kristofferson: "He's a walking contradiction, partly truth and partly fiction." He had grown up a Christian in Arkansas, but found it terribly difficult to adhere to his faith while being a major country music star. While he ached to be a good person, he spent seven nights in jail throughout his life on the road, spending one such night in the jail in Carson City, Nevada in the early 1960s. Indeed, Cash's appropriation of prison themes in his music can be understood as a representation of the sorts of limitations, burdens, and the desires that weigh on and confine the spirit, and the ensuing need for redemption and salvation in all human beings.

His role as a family man, especially when he was married to his first wife Vivian, also made him feel tied down. Johnny and Vivian had met while he was stationed briefly in San Antonio, Texas with the Air Force. They dated while he was there and continued a correspondence while he was stationed in Germany, where he would write the song "Folsom Prison Blues." Upon Cash's return to the United States, he and Vivian married, and they quickly started having children while he became increasingly famous as a touring musician. In Michael Streissguth's book, *Johnny Cash: The Biography*, Cash's daughter, Rosanne Cash, gives a poignant account of her father's reaction to the growing family. She said that her father was uneasy once their fourth child, Tara, was born. "When there's three," her father once told her, "they can form a circle around you and you can still get out. If there's four you can't get out."

Cash wrestled with himself throughout his entire life. His long battle with pills and alcohol are juxtaposed with his near-constant attempts to set himself straight with the God that he had dedicated himself to at a young age. The battle would take many forms throughout his lifetime, including his attempts at redemption through his prison shows and his failures ending in jail stints. Clearly, though, the battle was also manifest in the dark lyrics he created, particularly his famous line about shooting a man in Reno just to watch him die.

It is very telling that Cash almost always remained evasive when he was asked about that line in his song. He would make jokes when people asked him why the character in his song was stuck in a California prison after committing a heinous act in Nevada. He would speak broadly about the influence that the movie, *Inside the Walls of Folsom Prison*, had on him when he sat down as a young man to pen the lyrics. He clarified repeatedly throughout his life that he had never shot a man, nor had he spent time in prison. Aside from his brush-off response in the *Rolling Stone* interview, he really makes only one attempt to lend some finality to the questions that followed him for his whole career: "I'm sorry about this," he writes in *Cash*, "but that line in 'Folsom Prison Blues,' the one that still gets the biggest rise out of my audiences, especially the alternative crowds—'I shot a man in Reno just to watch him die'—is imaginative, not autobiographical." Perhaps trying to placate those who want even more of an explanation with respect to his process, he concludes with this: "I sat with my pen in my hand, trying to think of the worst reason a person could have for killing another person, and that's what came to mind. It did come to mind quite easily, though."

His answer offers little explanation of the inspiration that provided for the most famous line of his career. It provides little clarity as to why he had decided to write about such a terrible and violent act, especially given the state of American culture in 1955 when the song was released. Even if this answer, as well as his regular admission that *Inside the Walls of Folsom Prison* was involved, sheds some light on Cash's creative process, it does not begin to answer another very important question: Why did he choose Reno as the place where such an act would be committed?

The question is important because of the way Reno has become inextricably linked to Cash throughout his entire career. Many people all over the world know of the city because of "Folsom Prison Blues." Reno has enjoyed a dark and edgy reputation since Cash first recorded the song, especially since he re-recorded the album live in front of the prisoners at Folsom State Prison in 1968. And Cash has benefited from the icon he created as well: Solidifying the city's image also solidified his reputation as the original country music outsider over the five decades of his career.

Although Cash's explanation appears to be an attempt at a definitive resolution to the Reno questions that followed him, it is strikingly shallow and coy when one considers that the Reno line is the most famous and career-defining lyric in his body of work. Cash's vague and flippant responses betray the deeply private demons that inspired the choice of writing of such a base and evil act in Reno and might also point to legal reasons for avoiding clear attribution for the Reno line itself.

To understand why Cash chose to write some of the most chilling lyrics in American music, it is important to understand where he was in life when he wrote them. After leaving Dyess, Arkansas as a young man, he spent time in Pontiac, Michigan; Biloxi, Mississippi; San Antonio, Texas, and he eventually found himself stationed at Landsberg Air Force Base in West Germany. Germany was where he found his freedom for the first time, where he started to grow into his own, and where he would eventually write the song "Folsom Prison Blues."

Yet the geography of his relatively light travels only begins to describe the breadth of his life's voyage. On their face, his travels tell of a poor country boy who wanted to get away from the farm and his family by pursuing factory work in the North and military service around the world, two of the few options available to someone at his place and time. His travels also suggest that he was a man fascinated with being on the move and willing to pursue any option available to him to do so. They do not, however, seem to have anything to do with his decision to write his astoundingly dark lyrics, or to choose Reno as the location of them. He had never spent time in Northern California, the home of Folsom Prison, or in Reno when he penned the lyrics—but he had watched a man die. The painful and personal loss of his beloved brother Jack, who died in May of 1944, happened right in front of his eyes, and he carried the loss with him for the rest of his life.

To the young man destined to become a country music legend, his brother Jack was sort of an saint, representing everything he wanted to be: faithful to God, serious, diligent, and everything else that would have made his parents proud. Cash recounts his relationship with his brother as a way of depicting his own struggle with faith in his first autobiography, *The Man in Black*. Although a very personal autobiography, the book is actually best understood as a hagiography of his brother Jack, whose memory was sanctified by the family and kept as a personal measuring stick by his younger brother, Johnny.

The book starts and ends in homage to his brother. He begins by telling of Jack's devout Christianity, his intention of becoming a preacher, and of the seemingly special relationship that Jack had with their father. He concludes by stating that he will see his brother later, suggesting that he will win his battle on earth and meet him in Heaven. In the body of the book, Cash details his own struggle with fame, his struggle with drugs and the temptations of the touring star, and of his near constant struggle to bring God back into his life.

As has been recounted by biographers, filmmakers, and Johnny Cash himself, Jack died in a woodshop accident. He was cutting up wood with a table saw to make three dollars of much-needed extra money for the family when he slipped, slicing his fingers and his stomach badly. Cash describes the story in excruciating detail.

Survivor's guilt does not begin to explain what he must have felt after losing his brother. Perhaps telling of the way he viewed himself in contrast with his brother, Cash recounts that before the incident, he tried his hardest to persuade his big brother to put off the chore and go fishing with him. His brother's fastidiousness prevailed in Cash's memory, stating that he needed to fulfill his word and his obligation to the family. Even worse, while Jack was in the hospital room, Johnny had to be tracked down by his father, which must have only solidified the notion in the boy's mind that he was not fit to carry Jack's sandals.

The description of Jack's stay in the hospital for days is painful to read. Jack appears to be recovering, then succumbs to infection and other factors. As he lay dying, Jack recounted to his mother that he was having visions of going to Heaven and that he had to explain to God that he was not supposed to be in Hell. And then he dies. It was a graphic description of the future musical icon watching someone die for the first time and feeling trapped by helplessness and despair.

It is clear by the amount of writing and music Cash dedicated to Jack throughout his life that he had an enormous impact on him. One could conclude that Jack's saintly image in Johnny's mind was due to the rough road that fame and fortune took him on and his constant desire to be more like the brother he remembered. But that conclusion only forms half of the picture. His desire to be like his brother neatly explains what was on Cash's mind throughout his amazing career, but it does not explain why he cherished the memories of him so much, or if Jack's death might have played a role in his choosing to write those dark lyrics as a young airman in Germany. Streissguth's *Johnny Cash* is one of the best-researched histories of Cash's life and offers the best analysis of the demons in Cash's psyche. Specifically regarding Jack's death, Streissguth writes that Johnny "adored [Jack], finding in him a gentle father figure."

Cash's need to have a gentle father figure in his brother was so much more important because his relationship with his real father was ultimately frustrating. He clearly revered his father, stating near the beginning of *The Man in Black*, "I don't believe a man ever lived who worked harder and was more dedicated to providing for his family than my father, Ray Cash." And later, "I have good memories of my daddy when I was a little boy. I always thought he was about the greatest man I ever knew, and still do." However, while he expressed such sentiments towards his father, and clearly wanted to be loved and respected by him as well, their relationship was complicated.

Throughout his many interviews and his two autobiographies, Cash stayed pretty quiet about his relationship with his father. He suggests that he was a hard man, a veteran of World War I, trying to scratch out an existence and raise a family on a hardscrabble farm in Arkansas. At times he would suggest that his dad probably drank too much, succumbing to the pressures of being a provider during the Great Depression. Cash was probably more like his mother, whom he lionized in his writing almost as much as he did Jack. He took comfort in her spirituality too, often taking the form of hymns which he credits for his love of music. Being more like his mother, and probably indentifying more with her too, he seems to have never really fulfilled his need for fatherly approval.

Though he has been relatively quiet about his relationship with his father, details have come out. What he has said in various media is only augmented by what he has chosen to stay quiet on. Perhaps the most illuminating aspect of this relationship came after his death, when members of his family felt more free to discuss the issue openly. Streissguth's book captures an extraordinary quote from Kathy Cash, Johnny Cash's daughter. "Grandpa always kind of blamed Dad for Jack's death," she says. "And Dad had this, just real sad guilt thing about him his whole life," she went on. She then adds that her father told her, "One time when I was little, my daddy—he'd been drinkin'—said something like, 'Too bad it wasn't you instead of Jack.'" When she comforted him, he responded by saying, "Yeah, I think about that every time I see him."

No doubt this haunted him. No doubt this admission, coupled with the love of his much admired brother, led to many of the demons that he fought for the rest of his life. It is such a strong and deep affliction that it could possibly begin to explain what Cash was carrying with him when he left home for Germany, and when he sat down to think of "the worst reason a person could have for killing another person."

Cash tells a poignant story of his time in Germany that would have roughly coincided with his writing of the famous Reno line—one that depicts his inner conflict with wanting to live like his brother, yet at the same time, wanting to prove his father right in his estimation of him. After settling in to his new life in Germany, he seemed to have taken full advantage of the strange freedom the military offered to rural farm boys by drinking and carousing and otherwise enjoying the prestige of the Allied victory on the streets and with the women of rural Germany. However, the freedom offered a powerful reminder of his guilt too, as Sunday mornings in the peaceful country hamlets remind him of who he was supposed to be. He was supposed to be a good kid, a clean Christian from the Bible Belt, the loving younger son of a family that was just surviving in the dirt of Dyess. But he was not that kid anymore. When he watched the movie, *Inside the Walls of Folsom Prison*, he probably identified with the prisoners depicted in the movie: He was locked inside a game he couldn't win, with anger and frustration hitting him if he ran one way, and sorrow and guilt hitting him if he ran the other.

In his early twenties he was finally a free man. Though often confined to a set of headphones and military regimentation during his day job as an Air Force radio operator in Germany, he was free from the rigors that had accompanied his life in Arkansas. He was free from the toil in the cotton fields under the hot, harvest sun. He was free from the strained relationship he had with his tough father and the religious expectations of his devout mother. Perhaps most importantly, he was free from living under the shadow of his brother Jack, the "good son," who raised expectations for the rest of the siblings, and probably most especially raised Cash's expectations of himself.

Between Cash's experience of watching his brother die and the tumultuous relationship with his father and his faith that would follow, the picture becomes more clear of where a young Johnny Cash was when he wrote those words in Germany. He was shattered by watching his brother die. He was torn further by his need to fulfill his brother's spirituality on earth and by his father's statement suggesting that he wasn't any good anyway. He was trapped by his demons and his angels, pleasing neither, and enjoying the fruits of freedom only trapped him further. At this low point in his life he penned those powerful words. He never had to go to Reno to know that it was a place where such things were done. But he chose Reno because, in his mind, it was the perfect place to kill a person for no reason at all.

If this description of the internal struggle that could have possible permitted Cash to write those dark lyrics is accurate, then he had plenty of reasons to stay quiet about them. These are intensely intimate details, especially for a person whose personal life was so sought after by fans and journalists alike. One can understand why Cash would choose to be evasive and even coy when asked about his most famous line on these grounds alone, but Cash alluded to other reasons throughout his many interviews as well: Legal issues surrounding the origin of the line and of the song might have encouraged him as well.

Grant Alden, of the now defunct alt-country magazine, *No Depression*, suggests that the legal issues surrounding the provenance of the song and of the line might have caused Cash considerable consternation. "That song has somewhat of a checkered history," he says, stating that the song may have been subject to a plagiarism suit resulting in Cash having to pay a substantial amount of money in compensation. Streissguth confirms Alden's conjecture in his biography of Cash by pointing out that in his later years, Cash told his friend, Marty Stuart, that he had reworked Jimmie Rodger's line "I'm gonna shoot poor Thelma/Just to see her jump and fall" (from "Blue Yodel #1 (T for

Texas)") into his "Reno line." Borrowing the line itself was just the beginning, Streissguth suggests, adding that "not satisfied with appropriating only from the Singing Brakeman, the airman also borrowed from a copyrighted pop song of the day, 'Crescent City Blues,' which was written and recorded by Gordon Jenkins," a song that Cash had on an album while he was living in Germany.

As Streissguth points out, Cash was seldom pressed to discuss the origins of "Folsom Prison Blues" to the reporters who were able to interview him, as most were far more interested in knowing whether he had in fact ever shot a man in Reno just to watch him die. He reveals that Cash confided in his manager, Lou Robbins, that he was worried about how Jenkins might react to his song, even though his former producer, Sam Phillips, had told him that he did not have anything to worry about regarding the legality of the song. However, after Cash re-recorded the album live at Folsom State Prison, the version that truly took him to the top of the charts, he was in fact confronted by Gordon Jenkins, with whom he would later settle with a figure "that approached one hundred thousand dollars," according to Streissguth.

If Cash's reticence on the subject truly was legal in nature, then his silence does indeed suggest that there might be a traceable lineage to his Reno reference beyond that which Jimmy Rogers and Gordon Jenkins may have provided. Perhaps the setting for the song came from *Inside the Walls of Folsom Prison*, the song's structure came from "Crescent City Blues," and the Reno line's structure came from Jimmy Rogers "Blue Yodel #1." If all of these elements of the song were derived from elsewhere, it is possible that his choice of Reno was likewise derived. While there are countless films, books, and magazine articles set in and about Reno prior to Cash's song, none offer a truly conclusive connection to Cash's song. However, there are at least two cultural references that could possibly fit the bill.

The first possibility is the song "Reno Blues," by the great Woody Guthrie. Written in 1937, "Reno Blues" was about a slick city lawyer who tried to steal the lady of a Reno "gun toting cowboy" named Wild Bill. When Wild Bill catches the two together after returning from the cold range, he murders the lawyer and the song ends. "Reno Blues" was itself a parody of another old folk ballad entitled "The Jealous Lover," writes Alicia Barber in the book *Reno's Big Gamble*. Rose Maddox later recorded it under its more well-known title, "Philadelphia Lawyer." Wild Bill seems to have a more direct reason for killing in Guthrie's song than the protagonist of Cash's song does, but the song seems to be the first folk tune to paint Reno as the sort of place where a man might commit such an act.

More significant than the similar way in which both musicians present Reno in their music are the similarities in who they were and the demons they battled in their lives, sometimes eerily so. Cash was the "poet of the working man," and Guthrie, the "Shakespeare in overalls." Both were raised in dustbowl states, Oklahoma and Arkansas, on either side of the Great Depression. Both experienced the tragic and devastating losses of their beloved older siblings at a young age. Both were raised under the influence of the old time singing of their mothers, and the Carter family loomed large in their individual musical upbringings. Both hit the road hard to chase their musical careers, found themselves in Los Angeles and in serious trouble with their wives and three children back at home, until, in Cash's case, the fourth child was born. Both engaged in political activism, struggled with their relationships with God, substance abuse, and with debilitating neural diseases.

The biggest overlap between the two might have been that both were also musical icons that met their height of fame in 1968. For Guthrie, over 20 years older than Cash, his music had not been more popular during his career than it was at the time of his death on October 3, 1967. Cash, who outlived Guthrie by three and a half decades, recorded his groundbreaking album at Folsom Prison three months after Guthrie's death and released it six months later.

1968 was the year in which both lost their authenticity with respect to their music: For Guthrie, 1968 was when being an outsider became cool, and people like Bob Dylan swooped in and started creating derivatives of Guthrie's style. For Cash, 1968 was when his reliance on amphetamines, an addiction that started in 1967, forced him into the mainstream of American music to sell albums in order to maintain his lifestyle. Luckily for both, they were able to regain their credibility: Guthrie through the historical significance of his music that is still appreciated by purists today and Cash with his rebirth during the all-acoustic albums for Rick Reuben at American Records in the mid-1990s.

Guthrie probably knew quite a bit more about Reno than Cash did when he wrote "Folsom Prison Blues." He almost certainly traveled through Reno while crisscrossing the United States by train, and the city seems to have had a big impact on him. Beyond writing "Reno Blues," the city also appeared in passing in a list of albums he wanted to record: "War Heroes of World War Two, Prostitutes and Gamblers, Outlaws and Inlaws, Me, You, Cars I owned, Reno Jail (each man a song),

Holidays Around the World, Paid in Full." He was stationed in Las Vegas with the Army at the time of the list, and never recorded either "Prostitutes and Gamblers" or "Reno Jail."

In the book, *Hard Hitting Songs for Hard Hit People,* a collaborative effort between Woody Guthrie, Alan Lomax, and Pete Seeger, Guthrie mentions Reno in the introductions to several songs. Introducing "No Job Blues," Guthrie says in his inimitable way, "You know, I remember the night I got throwed in the Reno jail for Vacancy. Well, I don't know—I didn't know it was against the law. Hell every rooming house in town has a sign out in the yard that said: Vacancy."

Referencing this particular passage, Hillel Arnold, an archivist for the Woody Guthrie Archives and a folk musician, remarks that "the common threads—jail, violence, drug abuse, relationship between class and 'justice', etc.—in Guthrie's writing and 'Folsom Prison Blues' are, quite frankly, almost a little spooky." He is correct to point this out. The similarities in their lives are glaring, and the similarities in their songs about Reno are instructive as to who both musicians were. They were hugely important musicians for their times, extraordinary in their contributions to Americana. They were troubled souls, personally, spiritually, and physically, and figuratively, they were pretty clearly fellow travelers on the road to Reno.

Fiction offers a second possibility for Cash's knowledge of Reno, and yet, as with the possibility of "Reno Blues" above, the evidence remains inconclusive. Walter Van Tilburg Clark, a famous Nevada author, penned *The City of Trembling Leaves,* a coming-of-age story set in Reno from about 1925 through the early 1940s, which was published in 1945.

"This is the story of the lives and loves of Timothy Hazard, and so, indirectly, a token biography of Reno, Nevada, as well," the narrator says near the beginning of the novel. Tim Hazard is a composer of songs about Nevada who earns his living playing his music in the Reno honkytonks. It is the story of the dualistic battle between Timothy Hazard and himself. He is an unabashed dreamer trying to make amends with the reality and the realists of the world surrounding him; he is desperate to be loved, and self-loathing when his desperation yields sundry, but empty returns; he is a transient at heart, locked into the city he loves, Reno, the city of trembling leaves; and he is a talented musician, destined to write great music about Reno, but trapped writing popular folk, jazz, blues, and country music for the dance halls of Nevada and California around the time of the Great Depression.

Many of the themes presented above can be found in Cash's life, and in the song, "Folsom Prison Blues." In the song, the juxtaposition of movement in rhythm with the stasis of the main character is a brilliant, if entirely unintentional, metaphor of the city of Reno. The character is obviously a rambler, a criminal tied to nothing but himself and his travels, and who is stuck in prison. He hears the train—as does the song's listener—and it tortures him because he wants to keep roaming and living the life that pleases him. This is the essential story of Reno's early history. Established four years after Nevada became a state, Reno came to be because of its geography: Tramps from across the country came through Reno, the last train stop before crossing the daunting Sierra Nevada Mountains into California. Because of its Wild West nature, many of those ramblers lost their money gambling—or gave it willing to the ladies and barmen—and found themselves trapped against the mountains, while the trains rolled by tauntingly.

Clark perfectly captures a similar sadness and desperation in *The City of Trembling Leaves*: "The gigantic freight engines of the S.P., often two to a train when headed into the mountains, gently shake all the windows in the city in their passage ... . Their wild whistles cry in the night and echo mournfully all round the mountain walls of the valley. Thus Reno is reminded constantly that it is only one small stop on the road of the human world, that it trembles with the comings and goings of that world, and yet that the greatest cry of that world is only a brief echo against mountains ... ."

A deeper connection between the book and Cash's song can be found in their broad themes. In the passage that immediately follows that above, the narrator expresses the sadness that the trains evoke in a particular character, Mary, in language strikingly similar to that used by Cash in his song: "Mary once told me that the whistles of the big steam engines were so sad that when they woke her at night, in the bungalow on North Virginia, and she heard their echoes still slowly circling the valley and dying, she would sometimes even cry a little, and would invariably begin on long thoughts of loneliness and mortality." In this respect, *The City of Trembling Leaves* gives a paradigm for understanding themes of incarceration, the frailty of human life, and the uncertainty of justice that are so poignantly expressed in Cash's music. Indeed, Van Tilburg Clark's classic presents Reno as a microcosm of the tenuousness of the human condition—a living city revealing in itself the restrictions of human depravity and the possibilities of salvation and deliverance.

The City of Trembling Leaves was abridged and republished in 1946 as an "Armed Service Edition" and distributed to troops overseas. Even though it was abridged, both of the above passages were included in the "Armed Services Edition." Since Cash arrived in Landsberg, Germany around 1951, it is not impossible to imagine that he was able to obtain and read one of the abridged copies that remained after the invading forces, and several other iterations, left Germany. The simple fact that a book on Reno, in abridged form, was available to service members abroad does not provide any solid evidence for the claim that Cash may have received some inspiration from the novel. Yet it does seem significant, though, is that the content, themes, and even language used in both the book and Cash's song were so similar and that both revolved around Reno.

The City of Trembling Leaves is a classic among the coming-of-age novels set in the period of America's transition during the Great Depression and World War II. Given the cyclic nature of history, it is also timeless. It is the story of a man defining himself by defining his one true passion, in this case, music. It is the story of resolving the constant dualities that the enlightened, modern man faces in the honest pursuit of truth. And it is about the re-calibration of the human spirit that results from individual definitions and the reconciliation of the duality of man. Clark's popular depiction of Reno during this time, as well as the fictitious story of a honky-tonk musician, conflicted about the authenticity of his music, offers interesting insights and comparisons with real examples as well, specifically, the popular depiction of Reno by two of America's musical icons, Woody Guthrie and Johnny Cash.

Reno's general reputation in the 20th Century and its representation in the proximate influences on Cash's music traced out above suggest its image as a place of corruption and depravity into which human desire falls and confines itself. It is a kind of prison of which physical penal institutions are only vague copies. Cash's outreach to prison audiences throughout his life suggest an almost missionary zeal in showing others a path out of the confines of their prison and in seeking redemption himself—to show them, as he had found for himself, there was no fourth wall. ∎

The Politics of Higher Education:
Why the Nevada Board of Regents Should Be Appointed

JEREMY MCKAY

I. Introduction

Debates about the proper role and structure of Nevada's higher education system are an ongoing feature of public discourse in the State, and no debate arouses more controversy than that concerning the Nevada State Board of Regents. While most proposals to reform governmental institutions revolve around which design most enhances that entity's mission, disputes about the Nevada Board of Regents contain an additional element: As both a constitutional and an elected body, the Board of Regents embodies the American tradition of citizen oversight of its system of public instruction raised to the level of a constitutional right. Consequently, tampering with the Board's structure—especially the attempt to move from an elected to an appointed Board—seems to imply that a fundamental right of the citizenry is being taken away or at least compromised.

In this essay, I examine the question of the proper role and composition of the Nevada Board of Regents as the Legislature has taken up this question in the time since the *Nevada Constitution* was ratified. Unlike almost every other governing board in the State, this question cannot be decided solely in utilitarian terms, that is, merely by assessing which arrangement is most conducive and efficient in promoting postsecondary achievement among the residents of the State. Due consideration must be given to the Board's constitutional status, which is an original provision of the state constitution, as well as to the Nevada Supreme Court's decisions affirming the Board's exclusive administrative and executive control of the Nevada System of Higher Education.

A review of the institutional history of the Board of Regents reveals the array of concerns that have arisen in connection with the Board and the grounds for the various legislative proposals advanced in

---

Jeremy McKay is an independent researcher living in the Reno-area whose interests include Nevada political history, education policy, and topics related to the design of governmental institutions.

response to these concerns. Such a review yields evidence in favor of three main conclusions: First, as it is presently constituted, the Board of Regents is not designed to provide a unified and vigorous promulgation of higher education policy. Second, constitutional considerations notwithstanding, the Board of Regents would function more effectively as an appointed rather than an elected body. Third, such appointments should be gubernatorial rather than legislative or some mixture of the two. While these changes would require an amendment to the *Nevada Constitution*, they do not imply that the Board will lose either its independence or its constitutional authority. Rather, such a proposal envisions that a Board constituted in this manner would benefit from the "energy in the executive" branch, which, as has been said, "is a leading character in the definition of good government."[1]

II. Institutional History: 1864-1905

The Nevada Board of Regents appears to be unique in the nation, not merely in that it is the only elected governing body in state systems of postsecondary education, but also in that its composition through election is constitutionally mandated. Indeed, up through the first half of the 20th Century, most states had no statewide agencies overseeing their universities and colleges.[2] Beginning in the 1960s, most of these boards were created by ordinary statute to oversee the accelerating growth of their postsecondary institutions with the result that today 49 states have some body analogous to the Regents, the only exception being Vermont.[3] Of these 49 states, only Michigan has an elected board, which is also a constitutional body, but which is merely a coordinating board that oversees K-12 education as well. Of the rest, the vast majority of 31 states are composed solely by gubernatorial appointment; the board of one state, Wyoming, has entirely *ex officio* membership; the boards of two states, New York and North Carolina, are elected by the legislatures; and the other 12 state boards are composed through some combination of gubernatorial appointment with some provision for *ex officio* membership or legislative appointment.

It was the clear intent of Nevada's constitutional convention for the State's postsecondary governance system to enjoy a relatively high

---

[1] See *The Federalist Papers*, Federalist #70
[2] See *Reflections on Postsecondary Governance Changes*, Aims McGuinness, Education Commission of the States (2002), available through www.ecs.org.
[3] See *State Comparisons—Postsecondary Governance Structures Database*, Education Commission of the States, also available through www.ecs.org.

degree of governance authority and autonomy from both the legislative and executive branches. As ratified in 1864, Article XI, Section 7 of the *Nevada Constitution* creates "a Board of Regents to control and manage the affairs of the University and the funds of the same under such regulations as may be provided by law," and it gives authority to the Nevada Legislature to provide for "the organization of the Board of Regents, including, but not limited to, the number of members of the Board of Regents and the qualifications and terms of office ... ." But despite the fact that the members of the Board of Regents have always been elected, the mode of their election has varied greatly and the alterations in the manner of election account for the principal institutional changes in the Board over the years.

1) *Ex Officio* Membership (1864-1869): At the time of ratification in 1864, Article XI, Section 7 of the *Nevada Constitution* provided that the Board of Regents was to be composed of the Governor, the Secretary of State, and the Superintendent of Public Instruction "for the first four years and until their successors are elected and qualified." As is well-known, the federal Morrill Act of 1862 established a program whereby states could apply for land grants for the purpose of establishing institutions of postsecondary education. The Nevada Legislature made such an application to Congress in 1866,[4] and again in 1873, and a state university was eventually established in Elko in 1874.[5]

2) Legislative Election (1869-1885): In 1869, the Legislature reconstituted the Board such that it would consist of three "electors" who would sit for four-year terms and who would be elected by the members of the Legislature itself during its regular session.[6] This

---

[4] See Ch. 104, *Statutes of Nevada* 1866, which was an omnibus bill envisioning the structures of the university system.

[5] See Ch. 85, *Statutes of Nevada* 1873. See also Ch. 5, *Statutes of Nevada* 1867, which relates to the land-grant for the university.

[6] See Ch. 80, *Statutes of Nevada* 1869. There was a curious, though ultimately irrelevant, difficulty with the election of the regents by the Legislature in 1869. In the 1871 Regular Session, the Legislature declared the 1869 election of regents illegal and voided it (see Resolution No. 23, *Statutes of Nevada* 1871). It seems that the first election of the regents had occurred on March 4, 1869, but the bill establishing that the regents would be elected by the Legislature did not officially pass until the following day, March 5, 1869 (Ch. 80, *Statutes of Nevada* 1869). Consequently, on March 8, 1869, Gov. Blasdel appointed a board due to the illegality of the election, and in 1871, the Legislature recognized the situation officially and sanctioned the Governor's actions. Thus, the regents for 1869-1870 were in fact gubernatorial appointments.

arrangement was slightly modified in 1881 to stagger the terms of the regents with one member elected by the Legislature during the 1881 Regular Session and two to be chosen in the 1883 Regular Session, and so on, alternating.[7]

As the plans for the state university system were being realized, the Legislature began to specify the powers and responsibilities of the Board of Regents. The 1875 Legislature clarified that the Board had "full power over the buildings and grounds of the university" in Elko as well as "full power to make all expenditures necessary for the benefit and improvement of the institution." The regents were also authorized to employ "at least one teacher" to serve as "Principal of the University," who was the first executive officer in the Nevada system of higher education.[8]

3) *Ex Officio* Membership (1887-1889): In 1885, the site of the state university was relocated from Elko to Reno,[9] and, perhaps envisioning it as a more effective way of managing the move, the Legislature returned to the earlier model of *ex officio* membership where the Governor, Secretary of State, and the Superintendent of Public Instruction were to serve as the regents until January 1, 1889.[10] Since all of these posts were elected at the time, there appears to be no perception of a constitutional issue being generated by this particular mode of election. In 1889, the Board would again be comprised of three electors with four-year staggered terms, although the regents would no longer be chosen by the Legislature, but would be elected "in the same manner as other State officers." Another provision of the same bill discontinued the practice of having the Board choose a Principal from among the faculty, and gave them the power of appointing a "President of the University, to prescribe his duties, and to fix his salary."

4) Elected Board (1889-1891): As the fully elected Board began to come into office, the 1889 Legislature created and put under the Board's control the Agriculture Experiment Station, which was the point at which the regents were given authority over more than one institution.[11]

---

[7] See Ch. 53, *Statutes of Nevada* 1881.

[8] See Ch. 76, *Statutes of Nevada* 1875. The wording regarding the principal of the university was somewhat ambiguous, and it was clarified during the 1877 Regular Session. See Ch. 106, *Statutes of Nevada* 1877. This was again reaffirmed in Ch. 72, *Statutes of Nevada* 1885.

[9] See Ch. 72, *Statutes of Nevada* 1885.

[10] See Ch. 37, *Statutes of Nevada* 1887.

[11] See Ch. 26, *Statutes of Nevada* 1889.

5) Mixed Elected and *Ex Officio* Board (1891-1905): Having envisioned a fully elected Board of Regents in 1887 and with vacancies beginning to be filled with the election of two members in 1889, the Legislature expanded the Board to five members in 1891 with three regents to be elected and the Governor and the Attorney General to serve *ex officio*.[12] The precise reasons for this action are not available as testimony records were not kept at this time. However, it is clear that such an arrangement would make the Board more subject to the direction of the executive branch.

From its statutory inception, the Legislature has shown consistent interest in monitoring the Board's activities. In 1873, for example, it required the Board to make a full report of its activities,[13] and, in 1901, it required that reports be made to the Governor.[14] But the Legislature also took it upon itself to conduct a physical inspection of the university site. In 1875, it established a joint special committee whose charge was to visit the site of the university, to inspect its grounds, to take testimony from it employees, and so forth,[15] and it empowered another such committee to visit the university in the 1877 Regular Session.[16] More strikingly, it institutionalized these reviews in 1895 with the creation of the Honorary Board of Visitors whose task was to meet annually and tour the university facilities.[17] The Board of Visitors was headed by the Chief Justice of the Nevada Supreme Court who served *ex officio*, and included fourteen other members, each appointed by the governor serving two-year terms.[18]

a) *State v. Torreyson*: In 1893, in one of the key Nevada Supreme Court rulings on the Board of Regents, *State v. Torreyson*, *ex officio* membership on the Board was declared unconstitutional and direct

---

[12] See Ch. 65, *Statutes of Nevada* 1891. Also Ch. 59 and Ch. 80, *Statutes of Nevada* 1891 clarify some powers and responsibilities of the Board.

[13] See Assembly Concurrent Resolution (A.C.R.) No. 3, *Statutes of Nevada* 1873.

[14] See Ch. 33, *Statutes of Nevada* 1901.

[15] See Assembly Concurrent Resolution 10, *Statutes of Nevada* 1875.

[16] See Assembly Concurrent Resolution 11, *Statutes of Nevada* 1877.

[17] See Ch. 42, *Statutes of Nevada* 1895.

[18] See also Ch. 116, *Statutes of Nevada* 1913, which changed the composition of the Board of Visitors and which is the last mention of this body I find in the *Statutes of Nevada*.

election by the voting populace was held to be mandatory.[19] The reasoning of the Court is based on two points: first, that the regents are constitutional officers, and second, that the Constitution explicitly requires a "mode of election" to choose them. Accordingly, the Court held *ex officio* membership on the Board is repugnant to the constitution since "[i]t would be just as legal to make a regent, either by act of the legislature, or appointment, or election, ex-officio governor, or attorney general, as it would be to reverse the process" (518)—a situation that is scarcely conceivable. Relying on previous rulings, the Court further held that the mode of election clause "can only be construed to mean elected by the people by ballot" (518) in a manner substantially the same as other constitutional officers. This of course excludes legislative appointment which could be—and from 1869 to 1885 was held to be—a mode of indirect election.

In essence, the Court's reasoning in *Torreyson* is a *reduction ad absurdum*. If constitutional offices, such as the regents, can be filled *ex officio* by other constitutional office holders, then any constitutional offices can be filled in this manner. But this cannot be the case in general; therefore, it cannot be the case specifically with regard to the Board of Regents. The *Torreyson* decision is thus premised upon the full acknowledgement of the Board of Regents as a constitutional body. Thus, by holding that the state constitution requires the Board to be composed through direct election, the *Torreyson* decision is the cornerstone of the regents' authority and the basis for all subsequent rulings establishing their degree of autonomy from the Legislative and Executive branches of government.

III. Institutional History: 1905 to Present

(6) Elected Board (1905-present): In the 1905 Regular Session, the Legislature again removed the *ex officio* members in accordance with *State v. Torreyson* and held that as of January 1, 1907, the Board would be fully elected with three "Long Term Regents" serving for four-year terms and two "Short Term Regents" for two-year terms, all of whom were to be elected in the manner of other state officers.[20] Yet, in 1917, the Legislature increased terms of all regents to 10 years with a plan for

---

[19] See *State v. Torreyson*, 21 Nev. 517 (1893). See also *Dickerson v. Elwell*, 73 Nev. 187 at 189, 33 P.2d 796 (1957). The same principle was reaffirmed in *King v. Board of Regents*, 65 Nev. 533 (1948).

[20] See Ch. 88, *Statutes of Nevada* 1905.

staggered implementation of this increase when state elections were held in 1918 and 1920.[21]

It appears that 1917 saw a significant change in relations between the Legislature and the university system when Assembly Joint and Concurrent Resolution (A.J.C.R.) 1 was passed calling for an "investigation into improprieties of university management." This investigation was apparently conducted during the course of the 1917 Regular Session, since it was officially accepted by the Legislature in Senate Concurrent Resolution 17 of the same session.[22] Again, in 1939, the Legislature established a committee to investigate the university system in Senate Concurrent Resolution (S.C.R.) 21.[23] It was perhaps legislative suspicions or misgivings resulting from the 1939 investigation that motivated the 1941 Legislature to reduce the regents' terms from ten to four years.[24]

The period spanning the 1930s to the 1950s reveals an increasingly ambivalent attitude on the part of the Legislature toward the Board of Regents. On the one hand, the Legislature steadily increased the Board's authority: It transferred control of land in Reno directly to the regents;[25] it comprehensively clarified their powers and duties regarding the administration university;[26] and it empowered the regents to purchase land in Clark County for the construction of a southern branch of the University.[27] Also notable is the fact that no attempt was made in this period to return the manner of election of the Board to the earlier model of *ex officio* membership or legislative appointment. On the other hand, in addition to the investigation called for in S.C.R. 21 in

---

[21] See Ch. 189, *Statutes of Nevada* 1917. Ch. 52, *Statutes of Nevada* 1917 pertaining to the duties of the regents was also passed.

[22] See also Senate Joint and Concurrent Resolution 3, *Statutes of Nevada* 1917, which amends A.J.C.R. 1 (1917).

[23] See also Senate Concurrent Resolution 25, *Statutes of Nevada* 1939 which granted the committee a time extension to complete their investigation.

[24] See Ch. 68, *Statutes of Nevada* 1941.

[25] See Ch. 179, *Statutes of Nevada* 1931.

[26] See Ch. 229, *Statutes of Nevada* 1945.

[27] See Ch. 400, *Statutes of Nevada* 1955 & Ch. 27, *Statutes of Nevada* 1956. Also, the official name of Nevada's postsecondary system was changed in 1907 from "State University" to "University of Nevada" (Ch. 208, *Statutes of Nevada* 1907). In 1993, the name was again changed to "University and College System of Nevada" (Ch. 195, *Statutes of Nevada* 1993), and again, in 2005, the name was changed to "Nevada System of Higher Education" (Ch. 119, *Statutes of Nevada* 2005).

1939, the 1947 Legislature took the bold move of creating a parallel "Advisory Board of Regents" with rights of attendance at all Board meetings, but which had no rights to vote on motions before the Board.[28] It was the creation of this advisory board that precipitated the most significant court ruling to date concerning the Board of Regents.

b) *King v. Board of Regents*: The central Supreme Court decision that clarifies and affirms the Board of Regents' constitutional status is *King v. Board of Regents*, 65 Nev. 1948. As we saw, in 1947 the Legislature created the Advisory Board of Regents.[29] The cautiously worded statute created an ancillary board to "act in advisory capacity" to the elected Board that was to be invested with "all the rights and privileges … of the elected regents," except for significant restriction on the voting rights of the Advisory Board in that it was not to have a "determining vote on any matter properly under the control of the elected board of regents." The Advisory Board was limited to a maximum of seven members appointed by the Governor, but who were to be nominated by the elected regents. Furthermore, the act explicitly stated that the powers of the Advisory Board were not to be "construed in derogation of the constitutional authority of the elected Board of Regents to administer the affairs of the university." Yet despite these restrictions on the Advisory Board's authority, the Supreme Court held that such a body was unconstitutional and voided the statute.

The creation of a statutory Advisory Board attached to the elected, constitutional Board certainly appears to be questionable policy. Although the *King* decision focuses almost exclusively on the constitutional question, its reasoning seems to rest on the Court's determination that the Legislature's intent was for the Advisory Board to supplement, that is, to interfere, in some unspecified manner, with the elected Board's constitutional responsibility to govern the university system. In other words, the Court's reasoning seemed to be that if the Advisory Board was intended to have no substantive role in affecting the governance of the university, it could have no conceivable *raison d'être*.

Citing settled principles of Anglo-American jurisprudence and state constitutional case law,[30] the Court held that the Constitution's

---

[28] See Ch. 268, *Statutes of Nevada* 1947.

[29] See Ch. 99, *Statutes of Nevada* 1953, which repealed the statute establishing the Advisory Board. Also in 1947, the same year it created the Advisory Board, the Legislature required that all Board of Regents meetings be open to the public. See Ch. 244, *Statutes of Nevada* 1947.

[30] See *King*, 543 & 545.

positive grant of authority to the Board of Regents implied restrictions on the Legislature's ability to modify or interfere with its functions. Although the Constitution gives the Legislature power to "define the duties" of the regents, the same document gives the regents power to "control and manage the affairs of the university and the funds of the same," and so no ordinary act of the Legislature can "change, alter, or modify the constitutional powers of the board of regents." The Court held that an advisory board with "all of the rights and privileges" of the regular Board save the power of a "determining vote," would invade the Board's constitutional prerogatives, and once again, the text of the ruling seems to imply that such an advisory board could only be created with this purpose in mind, and thus its existence is unconstitutional. The Court also pointed out that the statute's language barring the Advisory Board from a "determining vote on any matter properly under the control of the elected board" was ambiguous since the definition of "determining" and "proper" was unclear and therefore might have actually allowed the advisory regents to cast non-determining votes in ancillary matters that were not under the elected Board's "proper" purview.

The *King* decision was brought forth from a statute born of the Legislature's intention to bring the Board under its influence without violating constitutional provisions. However, the opposite result occurred with the Court's strong affirmation of the autonomy of the regents and the degree of their independence from Legislative authority.[31] As the Legislative Counsel Bureau's legal counsel has succinctly stated, the Court held in *King* that the regents enjoy "exclusive executive and administrative control of the university."[32]

In 1955, the Legislature commissioned a further study to investigate the University, which was received in 1957 wherein the Legislature declared its finding that an "emergency situation" regarding the "administrative and academic operations of the University" existed.

---

[31] In his dissent, Justice Eather argued that the Legislature should be given a wider degree of latitude in regulating the Board of Regents because the distinction between "control and management" of the university, which the majority alleged to be constitutionally protected, and the regent's "duties," which can be "defined" through ordinary statute, is not at all clear cut. The majority opinion itself agreed that the framer's wording of Article XI, Section 7 is not ideal nor especially illuminating. See *King*, 565-567.

[32] See the Legislative Counsel Bureau publication, "Postsecondary Education," available at www.lcb.state.nv.us.

It further determined that this situation required that "the number of the board of regents ... be increased and that such increased number should be inducted into office prior to their election by the people."[33] Thus, in 1957, four members were added to the Board bringing its membership to a total of nine, and the newly appointed members served only until such time as they could be filled by election.[34] In 1959, for the first time, election districts were specified for the nine regents, with three to be elected from Clark County, three from Washoe County, and three from the rural counties.[35]

As was typical after the Second World War, the 1950s saw a renewed and steady expansion of Nevada's system of postsecondary education. In 1955, construction began on a southern branch of the University of Nevada,[36] and in 1956, the regents were empowered to purchase land in Clark County for this purpose.[37] By 1969, the southern branch was made a separate university with its own president.[38] The same bill also created the office of the Chancellor, who would be the chief executive officer of the entire university system.

c) *State v. Elwell:* As mentioned above, in 1957, the Legislature increased the number of regents from five to nine, citing an "emergency situation" at the university that required it. The four new regents were thus appointed to the Board until such time as they could be replaced in the regular election cycle. The peculiarity of the statute, however, was that the new regents were legislative appointees, not gubernatorial appointees, as is the usual practice with most state offices and which seems to be mandated by Article XVII, Section 22 of the state constitution. This statute precipitated *State v. Elwell*, 73 Nev. 187 (1957) in which the Supreme Court held that it was indeed within the power of the Legislature to create temporarily appointed offices in anticipation of them being filled in the next election cycle, but that the Legislature did not have the authority to fill those offices itself, a power reserved in the

---

[33] Assembly Bill 347 (1957) coming out of study in previous interim.

[34] See Ch. 122, *Statutes of Nevada* 1957. These 4 new members were legislative, not gubernatorial, appointments, and the Attorney General challenged the Legislature's right to do this, even on a temporary basis, under the state constitution, which precipitated *State v. Elwell*, 73 Nev. 187 (1957).

[35] See Ch. 78, *Statutes of Nevada* 1959.

[36] See Ch. 400, *Statutes of Nevada* 1955.

[37] See Ch. 146, *Statutes of Nevada* 1956.

[38] See Ch. 666, *Statutes of Nevada* 1969.

Constitution for the Governor. Accordingly, the Legislature's appointees were removed and the Governor's were installed in due course.

The *Elwell* decision was, in effect, a clarification of the Court's ruling in *Torreyson*, establishing that the Board could be filled through temporary gubernatorial appointments like all other state offices. Nowhere in the Court's opinion did the constitutional status of the Board of Regents enter into their reasoning, that is, the Court held that the Board is subject to the same legislative controls as other state offices vis-à-vis elections. The striking feature of the *Elwell* case was not so much the Court's opinion, but rather the extraordinary argument advanced by the Attorney General in contesting the practice of temporary legislative appointments. The Attorney General did not simply argue that such appointments were solely within the Governor's purview—which principle is clearly expressed in Section 22 of Article XVII and which was ultimately sufficient to win the case. More specifically, his argument was that "when a new elected office has been created by legislative act there is no power under our constitution to fill the office temporarily until it can regularly be filled by election …" (190), and, moreover, that if such a power were to be admitted, it could only belong to the Governor. The Court disagreed with this view since temporary appointments do not essentially alter the composition of the governmental body and so "the right of the people to an independent choice of constitutional officers" (191) is not compromised in such a case.

Clearly, the broader issue in the *Elwell* case was a dispute between the executive and legislative branches regarding their authority over the regents, and the Attorney General's argument evidences the lengths the former was willing to go in pursuit of its prerogatives. For if all elected offices had to be filled immediately by general election from the moment of their creation and no phase-in period through appointments or *ex officio* membership was allowed, the electoral machinery would probably be hastily and sloppily constructed and the electorate would have less opportunity to inform itself as to the powers and duties of these offices. In asserting executive control, the Attorney General was willing to ignore these legitimate governmental interests as well as the customary practices applying to other state offices.

In 1967, the Legislature raised the total membership of the Board to 11 requiring that five members be elected from Clark County.[39] However, in 1971 the Legislature reduced the Board's membership from

---

[39] See Ch. 191, *Statutes of Nevada* 1967.

11 to nine with the number of regents from Washoe County and the rural counties taken from three to two each.[40] The 1973 Legislature further refined the process of election and created electoral sub-districts from which each regent would stand for election, and the same bill held that, beginning in 1978, all regents would serve for six-year terms.[41] The Legislature's ongoing alteration in Board membership continued in 1991 when the membership was increased from 9 to 11 members,[42] and finally, in the Special Session of 2001, the Legislature set the number of regents at 13, where it remains to this day.[43]

    d) *Oakley v. Board of Regents*: In none of its decisions has the Nevada Supreme Court stated that the Board of Regents is a kind of fourth branch of government. But among postsecondary boards in the United States, the Nevada Board of Regents possesses a degree of autonomy akin to other constitutional offices whose essential functions cannot be modified through ordinary statute. A relatively minor restriction of the Board's autonomy was announced in *Board of Regents v. Oakley*, 97 Nev. 605 (1981), when the Court struck down a Board policy of mandatory retirement from the university system at age 70. The defendant, Chauncey Oakley, an instructor at Truckee Meadows Community College, contended that the Nevada System of Higher Education was not exempt from state law prohibiting discrimination among state employees on the basis of age. The Court agreed with Oakley, overturned the Board's policy, and wrote that the statute "does not appear ... in any fashion [to be] violative of our state constitution" precisely because the statute imposes a uniform obligation on other state, county, and municipal boards. In other words, the constitutional prerogatives and the essential functions of the Board were not compromised in this case because the statute did not single out the Board of Regents, but applied uniformly throughout state government. Thus, refining its earlier decision, the Court held in *Oakley* that "*King* ... does not stand for the proposition that the Board of Regents is free from all legislative regulation" (608).

---

[40] See Ch. 650, *Statutes of Nevada* 1971.

[41] See Ch. 183, *Statutes of Nevada* 1973. There was further refinement of the sub-district system in Ch. 730, *Statutes of Nevada* 1981.

[42] See Ch. 411, *Statutes of Nevada* 1991, which included alterations to voting districts.

[43] See Ch. 23, *Statutes of Nevada Special Session* 2001, which included alterations to voting districts.

In *Oakley*, the Court affirmed that the State law prohibiting the discharge of individuals due to age applied to the university system and that the regents were not excepted from any statute that "reasonably and properly impose[s] ... the same obligation that it impose[s] on other state, county and municipal boards" (607). However, the Court reiterated the core of the *King* decision stating that the Legislature "may not invade the constitutional powers of the Board through legislation which directly interferes with essential functions of the University" (608). Taken together, these two statements in the *Oakley* decision imply that legislation singling out and directing Board of Regents policy *is* legitimate but *only if* such legislation does not touch on "essential functions" of the postsecondary system. It is thus foreseeable that future litigation might test the limits of what these functions are.[44]

Although the judgment in *Oakley* was against the Board, the Court did not really depart from their ruling in the *King* case. As a matter of fact, the *King* decision itself specified that the Legislature had the right to "prescribe duties" to the regents so long as it did not impugn other "well-recognized legislative rights" *vis-à-vis* the Board.[45] Consequently, *Oakley* can be regarded as a refinement of *King* in that it helped draw the line as to what is an "essential" as opposed to a non-essential function of the State's university system in the specific instance of setting policy regarding retirement age.

IV. Proposals for Reform

As an elected body, the Board of Regents is a prime example of Nevada's political tradition of citizen government that is accessible and closely connected to the citizenry at large. For this reason, the Board possesses a certain democratic aura and legitimacy, which is difficult to articulate in precise legal terms, but which is apparent in every debate over its reform.[46] Yet even a cursory glance at the institutional history of the Board of Regents from the 1890s forward reveals that the Legislature has been unhappy with—and regularly attempted to find a more

---

[44] See *An Appraisal*, 48-49, which makes this same point with respect to the *King* decision.

[45] See *King*, 564-565.

[46] See, e.g., Regent Howard Rosenberg's comments in last session before the Assembly Committee on Education on May 3, 2007: "The fact is that the voters have the constitutional right to elect 'loons' and 'pinheads' if they want ... just as they have the right to remove them in the next election" (ellipsis in original).

satisfactory institutional arrangement for—the Board. Throughout the 20th Century, statutory changes have focused on expanding and shrinking the total membership of the Board and also on redrawing the districts from which each regent is elected. The increasing frequency of these actions testifies to legislative frustrations with the Board, and they also evidence the hope that a proper electoral arrangement will resolve them.[47] The Legislature has also attempted to oversee the activities of the Board more effectively through the creation of mediating bodies such as the Board of Visitors and the Advisory Board of Regents, the latter of which, as we have seen, was declared unconstitutional in the *King* case.[48]

No study touching on Nevada's higher education governance structure has concluded that the present institutional arrangement of the Board of Regents is adequate and should simply be maintained, even though the recommendations for reform have varied greatly. *The University of Nevada: An Appraisal* from 1956 cites the "needs for greater clarification of the constitutional powers and statutory duties of the Regents" and proposes a constitutional amendment to this end.[49] The 2003 report by the Committee to Evaluate Higher Education Programs,[50] while avoiding constitutional recommendations to modify the governance structure of the Nevada System of Higher Education, consisted of broad goals for the administration of the university system. These included the development of specific institutions and programs as well as the appointment of a legislative committee "to work with the Board of Regents to develop the Public Agenda for Nevada—that list of

---

[47] Legislative attempts to stop the ongoing fiddling with the number of regents have found expression in proposed constitutional amendments to fix or limit Board membership. See, e.g., S.J.R 10 (1959) and S.J.R. 8 (1961), both of which would have capped the number of regents at nine. See also No. 43, *Statutes of Nevada* 1957 & No. 27, *Statutes of Nevada* 1959 which held that the Board be composed of "not less than 5, but not more than 9" members.

[48] The creation of the Nevada Advisory Committee on Higher Education, the enabling legislation for which states that the need for "improved channels of communication with members of the legislature of the State of Nevada are desirable at all times," can be understood in light of the legislature's attempts to create ancillary bodies to supplement the activities of the regents. See Ch. 191, *Statutes of Nevada* 1967. Their system-wide report is available in the library of the Legislative Counsel Bureau.

[49] See Bulletin No. 28, *The University of Nevada: An Appraisal.* (hereafter: *An Appraisal*), Nevada Legislative Counsel Bureau, 1956.

[50] See Bulletin No. 05-3, which was called for by A.B. 203 (2003)

priorities that will guide strategic decision making about higher education in the State of Nevada" (14).

David Longanecker candidly summarizes the ongoing difficulties of the present institutional arrangement:[51]

> Recent activities by the Nevada Board of Regents reflect the unique difficulties that elected board members face, and thus the difficulties that such boards have in coming to a consensus regarding significant issues. ... [S]ome regents place the state's needs above the parochial interests of the specific communities and institutions, while others do not. As a result, historic battles between Las Vegas and Reno have impeded rational planning, regarding both research capacity and expansion of undergraduate education at the state's two major universities. ... Even when regents have worked together to move forward a positive agenda for the future, they have found it difficult to work with other critical stakeholders, such as the governor and legislature, because sharing power and decision making often feels like an abdication of their constitutional responsibility. (101)

The view that the Board of Regents is too "political" or "partisan" in the sense of being overly responsive to specific constituencies, and thus to narrow interests, rather than to long-term goals, is a frequent and historical complaint. Indeed, this was the conclusion of the Federal Bureau of Investigation, which, at the request of Governor Emmet D. Boyle, investigated alleged misconduct by Archer W. Hendrick, who served as President of the University from 1914 to 1917. Uncovering no wrongdoing on the part of President Hendrick, the F.B.I. recommended that Nevada:[52]

> ... take the control of its University out of politics. Until it does so no permanent improvement between the university and its constituency may be expected, nor will the university be able to furnish the leadership which the state requires.

The 1917 Legislature's decision to raise the terms of regents to 10 years was a direct result of these effects and reflected an effort to de-politicize

---

[51] See David Longanecker's "The New Challenge of Governance" in *Governance and the Public Good*. Tierney, William G. (ed.). State University of New York Press, 2006.

[52] As cited in *An Appraisal*, 17.

the Board.[53] Similarly, in 1929, when President Walter E. Clark was investigated by a legislative committee for allegations ranging from larceny and failure to supervise construction projects, to the dubious charges of opposing cheating and encouraging drunkenness, to the downright bizarre allegations that he had required female students to be photographed in the nude.[54] The findings of the commission fully exonerated Clark in every particular and pointed to a smear campaign for which certain regents were the principal agents.

The degree of constitutional autonomy of the Board of Regents has, unsurprisingly, led to a series of proposed constitutional amendments that would have altered the composition of the Board in such a way as to bring it under the control of the Legislature and/or Executive branches of government. The most recent of these attempts, Senate Joint Resolution (S.J.R.) 4, passed by the 2007 Legislature, but which failed during the 2009 Legislative Session, called simply for a Board composed through gubernatorial appointment without placing limits on terms or membership.[55] An earlier resolution, S.J.R. 20 (1967), also called for gubernatorial appointment, but it did not pass the Assembly. Yet unlike S.J.R. 4 (2007), most legislative proposals have envisioned some "mixed" type of Board. For example, Assembly Joint Resolution (A.J.R.) 11 (2003) would have created a Board filled in part through direct elections and in part through gubernatorial appointment while limiting membership to nine regents.[56] This resolution was passed again by the 2005 Legislature and became Ballot Question No. 9 in the 2006 General Election, but was not approved by the voters. Another

---

[53] See "Report of Joint Committee on Investigation of University of Nevada" (hereafter "Joint Committee Investigation of 1917"), in the 1917 *Journal of the Senate*, received on March 1, 1917, the 46th Day of the Legislative Session. See also *An Appraisal*, 17.

[54] See *An Appraisal*, 18.

[55] S.J.R. 4 passed the 2007 Legislature on a near party-line vote in the Republican-controlled Senate, with Republicans in favor and Democrats opposed. The Democratic controlled Assembly passed the measure 25 to 14 with 3 members abstaining. However, in the 2009 Legislature, the measure failed in the Democratic-controlled Senate, again, on a near party-line vote of 13 to 8 with two Republican Senators joining the majority—Sn. Nolan, one of the bill's sponsors, and Sn. Cegavske, both of whom had voted in favor of S.J.R. 4 in the 2007 Legislative Session.

[56] The number of elected regents would have been equal to the number of congressional districts in the State with the rest being appointed by the governor.

type of proposal has called for legislative appointment, such as A.J.R. 21 (1985) or A.J.R. 22 (1981), both of which were reported from committee, but failed to pass the Assembly. S.J.R 12 (1979) also called for legislative appointment.[57]

Committee testimony on S.J.R. 4 (2007) and A.J.R. 11 (2003) elucidates not only the central constitutional questions at stake in the redesign of the Board of Regents, but also highlights the different purposes served by gubernatorial and legislative appointment, respectively. The practice of gubernatorial appointment clearly intends to bring the Board within the Governor's policy making authority, lending a more unified, concerted, and energetic direction to the administration of the system of higher education. Put negatively, these proposals are premised on the legislative perception that elected board members govern in an uncoordinated fashion, focusing on short-term political ends rather than on the long-term development of the system and exhibit an unwillingness to submit to direction by the Legislature. These criticisms are not only explicit in the committee minutes, but have been the conclusion of official legislative studies.[58] In this respect, debates over the Board of Regents parallel those surrounding the State Board of Education,[59] and the Legislature seems now to have reached a

---

[57] See also A.J.R. 12 (1957) and S.J.R. 10 (1959) both of which would have allowed for either the election or appointment of the regents, i.e., it would have made the manner of the Board's composition an ordinary statutory question.

[58] See, e.g., "The Legal Position of the University of Nevada as an Agency of the Government of the State of Nevada" presented to the Legislature in 1963 by Frank C. Newman and available in the 1963 *Appendix to the Journals of the Senate and Assembly*, which is essentially premised on and repeatedly returns to the theme of the strained relations between the Board of Regents and the Nevada Legislature. In his "Final Comment," Newman makes an appeal to the relevant parties that "ALL QUESTIONS OR DISPUTES … CAN BE, AND MUST BE, 'RESOLVED IN THE BEST PUBLIC INTEREST'" (capitals in original) (47). Of course, if good government could arise from moral appeals alone, then little thought would have to be given to questions of institutional design. See also "Joint Committee Investigation of 1917," which constituents a strong indictment of the behavior of the regents on the occasion of the President Hendrick controversy. The recommendation found in *An Appraisal* was to amend the constitution to provide for an appointed Board of Regents in order to avoid the disadvantages of partisan politics arising from an elected board. See *An Appraisal*, 53-56.

[59] For a discussion of the Nevada State Board of Education, see Joe McCoy's "An Institutional History of the Nevada Board of Education," forthcoming in the *Nevada Historical Society Quarterly*.

consensus that making a more energetic and coordinated Board through gubernatorial appointment outweighs whatever good might be achieved through legislative appointment.

It is interesting to note that in the committee minutes, none of the opponents of S.J.R. 4 (2007) and A.J.R. 11 (2003) disputed their advocates' reasons for desiring an appointed Board of Regents. Rather, opponents of appointment tend to emphasize the abstract right of the Nevada citizenry to elect the governing body of its postsecondary educational institutions. Although citizens of Nevada do indeed enjoy this right, appealing to it begs the question in deciding whether such an arrangement should be continued or whether the constitution ought not to be amended to alter it. It is in this light that proposals for legislative appointment should be considered. The state constitution calls for an elected board, and from 1869 to 1885 their election was effected by the Legislature itself and not by the citizenry at large. Legislative appointment might thus be viewed as a compromise position that attempts to preserve the constitutional tradition of elected Boards, while providing a more effective selection mechanism than direct election and indeed one that would be likely to choose credentialed candidates. However, such a proposal still requires amending the state constitution, and it is highly questionable that regents appointed over many years by Legislative leadership or by the body as a whole would be sufficiently insulated from partisan considerations so as to be more apt to act in a unified, concerted way. In other words, the diffusion of responsibility in the legislative body of the Assembly and Senate significantly reduce the likelihood that any particular set of legislators would be held accountable for appointments to the Board of Regents. Consequently, such an arrangement would increase the likelihood of cronyism and lessen the effectiveness of the reformed Board.

Proposals for both gubernatorial and legislative appointments clearly share the ultimate concern of directing the administration of the postsecondary system through institutional design as opposed to budgetary mechanisms alone. Another type of proposal for reform of the Board of Regents avoids the question of the Board's composition and simply alters the constitutional provision giving the regents "control" of the university system. A.J.R. 42 (1975) would have altered Article XI of the state constitution to give the Legislature "control" of the university system leaving the Board intact to "administer" that system. This resolution, however, was not reported from the Assembly committee in which it was introduced. Similarly, S.J.R. 20 (1967) would have put "control" of the university in the hands of the Legislature, but still would have provided for gubernatorial appointment. The rewording of Article

XI of the Constitution to give the Legislature "control" would in effect override the *King* decision, but it leaves unanswered the institutional question. Even under Legislative "control," would an elected Board of Regents be the best means of "administering" the system of higher education? The Legislature—and probably the Nevada Supreme Court—would still have to return to the problem of distinguishing between "control" and "administering." Furthermore, another constitutional amendment would be required to address the "mode of election" clause in the same Article.

Another type of proposed modification of the system's governance structure has been to create more than one board for the various universities and community colleges in the State. A.J.R. 3 (1983) would have authorized a separate, elected board for the system of community colleges, but failed in the Assembly. Similarly, S.J.R. 13 (1979) would have created a "board of trustees" for the community colleges composed through legislative appointment. However, this resolution was not reported from the Assembly committee. A.J.R. 31 (1969) would have established two separate boards of regents, one for each of the two state universities, but was not reported from Assembly committee. No similar resolutions have been proposed for nearly a quarter-century during which time the university system has grown significantly in the number, and also in branch locations, of its various community colleges and Nevada State College has been added to the system. Consequently, it appears unlikely that such a proposal will arise in the near future. However, the institutional odyssey of the K-12 education system provides a cautionary tale. In this same time frame, the duties and the activities of State Board of Education have been supported and perhaps supplanted by a plethora of K-12 councils and commissions, all of which were created for specific educational goals formerly reserved for the State Board and all of whose recommendations the State Board are bound by law to adopt.[60] This in turn created a new set of institutional difficulties in which these councils and commissions operate independently of one another without sufficient coordination or even overarching supervision. Somewhat ironically, the 2007 Legislature created another council, the P-16 Council, to redress this situation, whose role, however, is purely advisory. In any case, there would appear to be adequate institutional experience to avoid creating a parallel situation at the postsecondary level.

---

[60] See ibid.

Taking a broader view of the issue, it is difficult to accept that debates surrounding the composition of the Board of Regents are ultimately driven by constitutional concerns. If postsecondary education achievement could be brought up to a high enough level within the budgetary restrictions the Legislature is responsible for imposing, it is difficult to believe the debate over the Board's composition would occur at all. The Legislature's attempts to exert control over the Nevada System of Higher Education are mainly born out of frustration with postsecondary achievement in the State and the Board's inability to improve this situation, rather than an abiding interest in usurping their legal role. The Nevada Legislature meets in biennial sessions and its Interim Legislative Committee on Education is largely devoted to researching educational matters and preparing policy recommendations for debate in future legislative sessions. To put it bluntly, the Nevada Legislature is not constituted in such a fashion to administer Nevada's higher education system nor has it shown an abiding interest in doing so. Opponents of a gubernatorially appointed Board are correct in affirming the constitutional status of the Board, but have never given an account as to why the unique circumstances of Nevada and its educational system require it. It certainly cannot be denied that an elected, constitutional Board is an institution peculiar to Nevada and cannot be said to enjoy any widespread basis in the education customs and practices in the United States as a whole as do, for example, local school boards at the K-12 level.

V. Conclusion

It is noteworthy that defenders of an elected Board of Regents do not make their case in terms of the effectiveness of such a governance structure, but rather in terms of the abstract right of the people to elect their regents. Yet in debates over reforming the Board, and specifically with regard to those proposals to make it an appointed body, this argument simply begs the question, since the *Nevada Constitution* prescribes mechanisms whereby the Legislature and citizens of the State can amend it. Unless proponents were willing to say that the practice of electing governing boards has the same status in American constitutional practice as electing legislatures, governors, and judges, then the effectiveness of the governance model should ultimately have priority over the constitutional question.[61] It should be further noted that,

---

[61] The Nevada Supreme Court's *Torreyson* decision can read as supporting this conclusion: *Ex officio* membership on the Board was held to be

barring a constitutional amendment that simply deletes Article XI, Section 7 of the state constitution, a gubernatorially appointed board would not lose any of its legal authority or constitutional autonomy.

The contrast between elected and appointed boards is typically described in terms of the former's representation of and sensitivity to public constituencies and the greater unity and directedness in the promulgation and attainment of policy goals achieved by the latter. But this contrast conceals the real issue at stake in the debate: How relevant are these functions to the primary aim of a state system of higher education, namely, postsecondary student achievement? The most that can be said in favor of elected governing boards is that they can be useful in exercising a kind of citizen oversight function with regard to agencies that serve important public goods, particularly in regard to providing scrutiny and enhancing the public visibility of budgets. But there is no evidence—and I find no individuals who make the claim—that elected boards are more capable of formulating policy and administering institutions so as to maximize educational achievement. The reason for this is evident: As a collective body, the voting public does not possess the specific knowledge required to choose individuals qualified for this role, and in general, democratic elections are not particularly effective means for constituting a board that is administrative in nature.

The main, non-constitutional argument offered against an appointed board is that the governor would be given too much power over the higher education system and so its degree of autonomy would be compromised. While this objection raises a serious concern, those who advance it do not realize that it concedes the major argument for an appointed board, namely, that gubernatorial appointments would be more effective in directing the Board's activities. Nevertheless, the argument is easily countered by the practice of staggering the appointments of regents, which would ensure that no single governor could dominate a Board through a majority of appointments. Thus, for example, a nine-member Board where a new regent is appointed every two years could never be stacked with a majority by a governor who is limited to two terms in office.

The direct election of regents by the citizenry is not conducive to the formation of a unified entity. But could the same be said of the

---

unconstitutional because, in theory, this would have allowed a regent to serve *ex officio* as Attorney General or Governor. If this result is an absurdity, it is only because the executive, legislative, and judicial branches are the core institutions of American republican government, whereas boards of regents are not.

Legislature itself? Could the present argument be taken to imply that legislatures are themselves unsuitable governing bodies as well? Taken as a possible objection to appointed board, this comparison misses the mark for two reasons. First, state legislatures are designed to represent a very broad array of interests among the citizenry and to exercise broad supervision over the whole apparatus of state government. Their purpose is not to provide management of highly specific arenas requiring a specific knowledge base. If legislatures were in general capable of this, then state agencies could simply be abolished.

Second, legislatures are designed to be as comprehensive of a wide array of interests and voices, and their operations are to some extent premised upon faction and conflict. However, most legislative bodies are possessed of their own internal mechanisms that lend a unifying tendency to the law-making process and that allow them to self-organize in ways that are generally intelligible to those who participate in them. Such mechanisms include the committee system, where chairmen possess a greater share of power than the others; the seniority system whereby those with greater tenure enjoy more influential positions; the caucus system and other means for enhancing and maintaining party discipline, in addition to a well-developed theory and history of legislative procedures and practices that inform the actions of individual legislators as to their duties and scope of action. To this list we could add features that are more difficult to quantify, but that clearly exert a strong influence on legislative activities: the prominence of individual members within the legislature due to their particular career and public service backgrounds; the importance of regional loyalties and sympathies that generate minor and so containable factions with the whole; the fact that a legislature's understanding of its role in government is generated by being separate from and often in opposition to the executive branch of government; the *esprit de corps* specific to an individual house of the legislature, etc. All of these features of the legislative branch are means by which faction and strife are not abolished, but directed and channeled in such a way as to allow for the institution to function as a kind of unit. There are, however, almost no analogues to these structures in the elected Board of Regents, whose successful operation must therefore depend upon the good offices of particular individuals who, in the best cases, are able to exercise suasion upon their colleagues to act and vote in certain ways on specific issues.

In the absence of internal, self-organizing mechanisms in the Board of Regents, the Legislature has tended to enact measures that impose control mechanisms on the Board aimed at directing its activities externally. Examples of this range from its ongoing changes to election districts and total Board membership to the 2005 legislative letter of intent redirecting fee collection. In 2007, for example, the Senate Committee on Government Operations agreed to an amendment temporarily depriving the Board of Regents of the ability to make legislative bill draft requests. The 2009 Legislature made this prohibition permanent.[62] If the Board of Regents were a mere statutory board, these legislative acts would be dubious and inconsistent with normal governmental practice, since it is the custom of the Nevada Legislature to grant bill draft requests even to certain non-governmental bodies. But depriving constitutional officers of the right merely to propose legislation is unprecedented and bespeaks a deep mistrust and indeed the will to act punitively vis-à-vis the Board. These measures demonstrate that, while the Legislature is constitutionally prohibited from interfering with what are deemed to be the "essential functions" of the university system, it seems increasingly driven to exercise control in peripheral ways. Thus, quite apart from the merits and good intentions of individual regents and legislators, the present institutional configuration almost necessitates a reciprocally confrontational relationship between these two bodies. This is not to say that attitudes cannot be overcome through the efforts of key individuals, but only that there exists a substantive obstacle that must be overcome in the coordination and direction of the institution.

Interestingly, the budget crisis beginning in the wake of the 2007 Legislative Session demonstrates the same institutional intransigence on the part of the Board, though in a salutary way. The series of budget cuts proposed by the governor, culminating in the proposal of an enormous

---

[62] See Amendment #1123 to S.B. 490 (2007), which was offered on June 2, 2007, two days prior to the close of the legislative session. Testimony notes reveal that it was explained as repealing an earlier amendment to the bill, and the substantive provision eliminating the Board's authority to make bill draft requests was not discussed. As noted above, this provision was to expire on June 30, 2011. However, Amendment #707 to A.B. 535 (2009) simply removed the sunset date enacted in S.B. 490 (2007). The text of the amendment, however, did not contain the full statute that was being amended. In other words, any legislator viewing this provision in the amendment would have likely understood it simply to be a technical, clean-up provision and not the indefinite extension of a prohibitive change. Tesimtony on A.B. 535 (2009) in the Senate Committee on Legislative Operations and Elections from May 14, 2009, refers generally to S.B. 490 (2007) "set[ting] limits on bill draft resolutions and required prefiling of state and local government BDRs." In sum, it is doubtful that, in either case, the majority of legislators actually knew that they were voting to end the Board's authority to request legislation.

36% cut to the Nevada System of Higher Education for the 2009-2010 biennium hardened the resolve of the Board of Regents and its Chancellor, inspiring a general unwillingness to cooperate with what would have resulted in crippling higher education in the State, probably for several decades. It is altogether fitting that the constitutional officers charged with administering and developing higher education in Nevada should take this stance. But this series of events also demonstrates the degree of threat to these institutions that is necessary in order to provoke the Board into a sustained, unified response. The lesson of history seems clear: In bad economic times, faced with reckless budgetary recommendations from a hostile governor, when the very fabric of the university system is at risk, the Nevada Board of Regents will function fairly well in opposing these forces. In good times, in developing and implementing long-term plans, individual and local interests along with an institutional resistance to any outside direction from the Legislative and Executive branches will dominate degrading the Board's ability to make meaningful changes.

The practice in Nevada of electing the Board of Regents is therefore a constitutional provision that has outlived whatever utility it once possessed. While there is a genuine argument to be made that a poorly functioning institution has some virtue merely in the fact that it is established, well-known, and broadly accepted, the social, economic, and the educational circumstances making up the state of Nevada require a Board whose members can be vetted for qualifications and chosen for their demonstrated understanding of and commitment to the educational needs of the State. The low educational attainment levels of students in Nevada are well-known, and Nevada's consistent low-ranking in comparison to the other states in the union is no more acceptable for being a well-known and persistent fact.[63] Less noticeable but probably more significant are the idiosyncratic features of Nevada's social life and cultural mores in which a cultural premium on educational attainment has not figured prominently, and of Nevada's economy, which historically has offered relatively high-paying jobs, but which has not required a highly educated workforce. Given these conditions, a Board whose principal activity is to represent constituencies—no matter how well it

---

[63] For an multi-faceted profile of Nevada's education trends and problems, see the presentation given by NSHE Vice-Chancellor for Academic and Students Affairs, Jane Nichols, before the Assembly Committee on Education on April 18, 2007, available through the Nevada Legislature's website at www.leg.state.nv.us.

fulfills that function—cannot be expected to provide the sort of sustained leadership and concerted control of the university system that is needed to improve these conditions.

The implicit social contract that lies at the base of Nevada's political life—maximal individual liberty and relatively little governmental regulation—has gone hand-in-hand with the peculiarities of its tourism industry and a willingness among its citizens to forgo a developed, state-administered social welfare network. These elements, along with a strong tradition of citizen, non-professional government, are at the heart of Nevada's understanding of itself as a polity. No structural reform of the State's governing institutions can disregard the temper of the laws that and the motivating spirit that fostered their development. What is at issue, however, is the preservation of Nevada's political tradition in the face of changing social circumstances—the transition from a primarily agricultural and mining based economy to a knowledge-based economy requiring a higher level of specialized training and cognitive skills that is integrated more thoroughly in the national and world economy. Such a transition could not be effectuated by a team of technocrats, who are ignorant of the social life and political history of the State, any more than by a group lacking the acquaintance with the mission of higher education and the knowledge-base sufficient to administer the system so as to fulfill those goals. While not a panacea for Nevada's educational challenges, the practice of appointing regents would be the best institutional structure for selecting a Board and moving toward these ends.[64] ∎

---

[64] Without attributing any opinion expressed in the above essay, the author would like to thank staff at the Legislative Counsel Bureau's Research Division and the Nevada System of Higher Education's Academic and Student Affairs Division for their kind assistance.

9/10

Brad Summerhill

She propped her breasts on the counter like a merchant showing off the goods, her palms sweeping to her face, manicured nails framing a sweet smile. His heartbeat quickened at the memory of Stacy's warm body pressed against his own soft body, a deep, affectionate hug on the first Sunday they churched together, just yesterday. She'd made it plain they had prospects. Like an anthropologist, Rusty Cisar witnessed her fellow congregants rocking and rolling in the aisles, black folks without rhythm, Latinos jumping for Jesus, white guys in golf shirts doing a St. Vitus dance. The sanctuary seated hundreds, more than enough room on the stage for a twelve-piece rock band: projected lyrics, worshippers' arms in the air, colored lights, a laser show, everything but dry ice. They hadn't spoken in tongues exactly but their bodies babbled aplenty. "Don't you love it," she whispered as the couple in front of them held up flaming Bic lighters.

She was ten years younger, divorced, adorable, and she liked him: all things considered, an incomprehensible situation. Since long before his own divorce Rusty had gotten used to celibacy, not at all used to the idea that there were women out there who might find him attractive.

A cuckoo clock tic-tocked behind her. Tiny Bavarian dancers celebrated the top of the hour at Alpine Bells Wedding Chapel with squats and twirls.

"You in a hurry, Rusty?"

Stacy had started as the receptionist several months ago. Rusty married people. She earned enough to live in a run-down studio in the university district. He earned enough to live in his mother's run-down bungalow near the river, the same house he grew up in.

"I have to see a friend," he told her. "He's ill. Not doing well. Needs some counseling."

"I'm so sorry, Rusty," she frowned. "Is it like last rites or something?"

Brad Summerhill is a writer who lives in Reno, Nevada. His short story, "Bring Her Back" has been published in the *Red Rock Review*. "9/10" is an excerpt from his forthcoming novel, *The Half-Life of Weddings*.

"No, nothing Catholic. He just needs some support." They were long-time friends, he told her. They'd built log cabins together back when they were deciding whether to evade the draft.

"Before you were ordained."

He paused, stuttered, "Stacy, I should tell you, I'm not born again or anything, you know. Never will be, I guess."

"I know that." She picked up the telephone, listened for a dial tone, set it back in its cradle, pressed the worn square buttons as if it were a calculator.

He had to go, he said.

"I'll be here," she said in a way that made him think there would be no second date.

He verified with Quan-Ping that his friend Mary would cover for him today and left through the kitchenette.

He'd let things in Gold Hill go on too long, three days since he spoke with Greg by phone. He last saw his friend before the Fourth of July wedding rush. On the telephone Greg muttered and mused, said everything was okay, joked, his usual self. Rusty feared he would never become his old self again. A year ago he talked suicide like checking groceries off a list.

He stopped home to check on Angelique, his mother. She and her new boyfriend, a no-good she picked up over summer somewhere in Florida in her old Jamboree, weren't home.

Things were still green along the Truckee River. Autumn crocus buds sprang from Mrs. Patterson's grass, the one yard on the block that was still cared for.

He toured down Arlington in his electric blue Geo Metro, watched the naked profile of Mount Rose as he merged onto the freeway. He was inclined to ascribe the snowmelt to global warming but figured his penchant for nostalgia might have put a false memory of an eternal cape of snow in his head. He drove south and turned away from Mount Rose for the Virginia Foothills. Three motorcycles clipped by on the winding two-lane highway to Virginia City, the last rider flipping him the bird as they grumbled round a curve, presumably in response to his cautious driving.

September air vented his hibiscus-splashed Hawaiian shirt as the road reached the ridgeline. Along C Street he puttered past tourist shops and wooden-planked casinos, drove through Virginia City toward the far canyon where he'd camped on a lot in the summer of 1971 building a house with Greg. Thirty years backward was his rate of travel as he arrived in Gold Hill. The road dipped across railroad tracks, fell to its nadir. He followed a looping gravel grade onto a hillock where an alarming cluster of vehicles barricaded the open double-car garage.

Larry Lufert's MG, top down, was trapped in sagebrush behind a Ford F250. *And we shall return to the place where we started and know it for the first time.* Lufert, a poet, often recited the line. Rusty got the feeling he hadn't written it but wanted Rusty to think he did.

The house, originally a single room with a loft, had become something bourgeois—"bourgeois" the exact word Greg would have used, conversant back then in all the requisite leftist theory. Everybody softens. Rusty softened in the middle. They kept pictures in the den: in one, a muscular Rusty, wild hair tenting his shoulders, burly arms burnt Kodachrome red, a thick chest and flat belly.

Ducking out of the Metro, he fought down a wave of nausea. Greg hadn't said it would be a party.

The garage was no longer cluttered. Things had been sold off or boxed up, stacked along the walls beneath high empty shelves. He realized later it was the first step in preparing the house for sale. Tyler Glenn's wife, Dahlia, stood in close conference with two women in the kitchen. They acknowledged Rusty, made way for him to pass into the living room, a bizarre space nearly the size of a gymnasium, knotted cedar covered by a series of three stretched canvasses, splashes of muted sage and blues, pieces of confusion trapped between landscape impression and abstract expression which Rusty never cared for, the work of a mutual friend. Greg's young friend Jason slapped Rusty on the shoulder, asking if he needed a cold one. Tyler Glenn and Larry Lufert shook his hand, returned to their thoughts. People he didn't know averted their eyes or stared past him. Walter Danforth, the sheriff, sat by himself in jeans and a rumpled short-sleeved dress shirt under the meridian sun in the far corner beside two plate glass sections of wall that formed the southwest corner of the huge room. The enormous windows under cathedral ceilings gave the sense that the room extended beyond the level westward rim of the canyon to the far Sierra horizon. Someone lit up a joint in one of the back rooms.

"Yeah," Lufert barked, "we all gotta kowtow one at a time like he's some fucking Persian demigod."

"More Roman I'd say," Tyler Glenn spoke in the slow, quiet drawl he'd cultivated for television. He switched his legs, hoisted a scuffed work boot over his thigh. "I'd say more Roman altogether." His lips pursed beneath his Mark Twain mustache.

"I see," Lufert lurched, "like an official decree, right? Cup of hemlock?"

Tyler Glenn ignored the poet and Rusty realized they were both soused. With a quivering hand he refilled Glenn's glass from the bottle of bourbon on the coffee table. Glenn told him to pour himself a glass then corrected himself, "Shit, that's right, you're on the wagon, eh? Don't know how you do it."

In fact, Rusty considered it a dubious decision. The black beauties were the near death of him. Alcohol never harmed him, it was the pills. He'd been pressured—by peers, by the court, by his ex-wife under threat of never seeing their son—to attend AA along with NA, to admit he was helpless, to put it all together in a package deal.

"I'm rationalizing," he said aloud to no one in particular.

"You are?" Lufert bellowed. "So am I. Just being here is rationalizing." He snatched the bottle from Rusty's hand.

The black lab, Floyd, banged into Rusty's knee, wanting attention. Rusty excused himself.

He checked for Stephanie in the garden. Gourds—yellow, green-speckled, white—lay under clumps of rough, twisting vine. Greg's old tractor sat beside an unfamiliar backhoe. He followed the flagstone path around the corner and saw the pinewood coffin set on saw horses, unstained, a lid leaning against it. He inspected it, couldn't help feeling the smooth wood, mesmerized. It was well built, perfect geometry, dovetail fittings at each end, no nails, definitely not Greg's work. Someone in there had built his friend a coffin.

He kicked his way through shoes scattered in the mud room, found her speaking to a woman he recognized but whose name he couldn't recall.

"Your sister's not here," he interrupted them, absentmindedly resting his hand on a dusty TV.

She brushed aside a ribbon of brown hair and a smile flickered across her face, her eyes red-rimmed, all else pale, drained, the expression of a widow at a wake, which part she acted and in doing so in Rusty's estimation making it real, making it come into being. She hugged him politely. "You know she couldn't be here." Her shoulders hunched forward as they did when she was a self-conscious teenager taller than the boys.

"She doesn't know anything about it? She wouldn't stand for it, would she?"

"No, I left Kate out of this one."

"This is insane. You didn't think to leave me out too?"

"I wanted to," she fixed her dark eyes on him. "Greg wanted you."

The woman touched Stephanie's shoulder. Stephanie told her it was okay and she slipped away to the main house, up a sheltered staircase toward a sunlit landing, this lower portion of the new house dug out against the old foundation. Stephanie spent her time down here toiling at watercolor paintings she never showed to anyone or out back gardening in the makeshift greenhouse Greg had built for her.

He'd had a crush on her. Rusty flattered himself to think she took her time deciding between himself and Greg that first summer at Tahoe. He believed it was true and didn't care if it wasn't, a private notion almost unconscious, a fixed idea that helped him become himself. They'd met on the doorstep of adulthood, childhood just behind them, their true selves hidden ahead within unseen rooms. That Rusty could have become an ordained minister—even a skeptical, non-evangelical one—wouldn't, couldn't have occurred to any of them back then, least of all to Rusty himself. Angelique was still waiting for her fifty-year-old son to find a real job, couldn't comprehend the path he chose. Greg and Stephanie shared her incredulity. Greg's ridicule and Stephanie's scorn—or was it pity?—were to be expected. He never doubted their friendship.

"I thought it was supposed to be an intervention," he said.

Stephanie rubbed her palms over her swollen eyes, spoke from behind her hands. "He's tired of it, Rusty. It comes on him every day more and more. I couldn't believe it either. He wanted to let you think it was counseling, fucking intervention, whatever you call it, said it was the only way to get you up here." Her sad, green, bloodshot eyes narrowed into focus. "He says you're a coward."

"No question about it."

He wished he hadn't responded so quickly.

"This isn't easy for me either, you prick."

His sore knee barked at him as he trailed her up the stairs to the sunlit landing. He yelped, clutched his kneecap. She kept moving. Four friends sat stoned in the backroom, a diffusion of pot smoke curling over the crown molding. Two girls on a futon held hands, tears streaming down their cheeks. Before she lost herself in the gym-sized living room, Stephanie turned to him, hissed, "It has to be serene. Please understand. He's counting on you, Rusty." She moved as if to touch his shoulder. "He's counting on you," she repeated, more calmly, and walked away.

Walter Danforth watched their two-step. Rusty crutched along the back of the couch toward the recently reelected Storey County sheriff, limped across a wide sage and blue carpet to the far end of the room.

"Leg hurting you, Rusty?"

"You're risking your career, Walt."

Danforth offered no reaction. "Not much of a career anyway," he said finally. "Tyler Glenn warned me." Glenn had been sheriff when Rusty and Greg arrived in Gold Hill in 1971, before he became a television personality.

"They say it's an inherited office," Danforth went on. "You know that, being from here and all."

"No one's from here, Walt, people just live here."

They moved onto the patio. Yellow tailings hung like sick tongues along the rim of the pockmarked canyon, exit holes of played-out veins. Rusty could faintly hear bleeping, the guttural roar of an industrial-sized diesel engine, a cement quarry down the road the only trace of mining left on Mount Davidson. More poets than miners resided in the ghost towns surrounding American Flat.

"I don't like it either, preacher, but it's what the man says he wants to do."

"He wanted it to look like an accident last summer. Wanted me to walk him down the Savage, leave him for dead."

Danforth shrugged, knew nothing about it.

"It's illegal and you can't let it go on, Walt."

"No, Rusty, he cleared it with the county." He waited for Rusty's face to unfrown itself. "It's hospice care. Don't," he said, "I had nothing to do with it. I'm dead serious." He grimaced. "Forgive the expression."

After seminary Rusty had done hospice care in Oregon. He'd seen euthanasia at its best, its worst. "I thought this was an intervention. We had time."

"Intervention?" Danforth grinned. "What the hell?"

"Time, I told him. I said give it time. Shit, one more spring. Who wants to die in September?" A gust flapped the end of his silk shirt. "Who can say when your last good day has come and gone?"

"And you're going to talk him out of it."

"If I can."

Danforth grunted. "You think he hasn't thought it through?"

"How can he think it through? That's my point, Walt. He needs his friends to do something. Not sit around glugging a bottle waiting for him to commit suicide."

"And you want me to go up there and arrest him."

Rusty looked over. "Can you do that?"

Danforth brushed his mustache. "There's nothing criminal going on here, Rusty. Except those potheads back there."

"And you're not on duty anyway?"

Danforth nodded, as if deciding the issue. "I won't be here if something illegal does go on. So far it's aboveboard. People do things we can't comprehend. You gonna ruin me, Rusty? Go ahead. There's nothing in state code says what 'terminally ill' means. I looked it up. And the planning commission made a positive recommendation to the county board on Greg's hospice care."

"They call it hospice care? Since when?"

"Over summer. You know as well as me he's friends with all those people. I would've thought he told you. Sorry. I won't be here, Rusty. I'm going up there talk to him. I won't say goodbye. That's as much as I can promise." He grabbed Rusty's arm. "I'm with you more or less, Rusty, but I don't know what the hell you want me to do. Ten years I've known him."

"You'll say something to him? Talk him out of it?"

Danforth sighed. He brushed his mustache, twisted, leaned on the railing. "I don't know what I can do. Hell, I'm still not convinced it's not another performance of his but if the crazy bastard goes through with it, I don't want my last words with him to be words of conflict. That wouldn't set right. Do you see?"

Rusty felt a slow immersion into an amber dreamworld, the edge of vertigo, thoughts and motions disconnected. "I need help, Walt. It's like you say, I can't stand up there alone."

"I guess he thought it through, Rusty." He squinted at some far point down the canyon. "Crazy fuck. I told him they might find a cure."

A hawk banked into view above them and disappeared behind the roof.

"Know what he said?" Danforth snorted. "Said he'd found the cure."

"But we don't get to choose, do we?"

"My own cowardice would prevent me. Georgia won't be here today, said it was a matter of conscience. I'm so yellow I couldn't even stay away. Greg whistled and I come trotting." He hung out his tongue like a faithful dog which didn't mask his growing sullenness. "Yellow lab," he said, "that's me. Good buddy for Floyd."

Greg's black lab was sniffing around the unfamiliar backhoe. The setting sun cast an orange glow on the treeless hillocks. Rusty wanted to call Greg outside to see the day's last, most beautiful light. As if in response to his thoughts people gathered at the glass wall behind him. Stephanie made her way forward. There was a noise above of a sliding glass door and slow, heavy footsteps. The outline of legs, a fat belly and a walking cane could be seen on the upstairs patio through the redwood planks. The afternoon clouds massed over the canyon slowly purpling while the broken, billowy blanket hanging over the Sierra took on iridescent edges, the sun for a moment visible underneath the cloud cover, the dim afternoon lit to brilliance. He thought he heard Greg speak. He wanted to call to his friend but felt as if he were mute or would find himself mute were he to move his tongue. A high thick contrail gleamed in an open patch of sky. A burst of prismatic light punctured the silence, a moment so luminous, so colorful, it seemed artificial—the green work of an art school hopeful.

"That's all, folks." Greg's voice broke over the breeze, giving Rusty hope it was all a vulgar performance. The worst jokes Greg loved best.

The sun dropped, gloom crept over the house and Rusty found himself alone, the people at the glass wall gone, Greg gone, Walter Danforth no longer standing next to him. Only an eye blink and he was alone: time travel rather than the presage of dementia a man Rusty's age might fear. More than once before the morning light he would travel across the years, no simple nostalgia but the displacement of his entire being.

Jason startled him with another offer of beer. "I'll be in the yard when they need me."

"You saw Greg?"

Jason removed his ball cap, wiped his forehead, bald in his late twenties, a reddish tinge to his sideburns and goatee in the failing light. Jason had become a close companion of Greg's, ridiculous for Rusty to feel jealous of the association as if they were all fags in a love triangle, but it angered him suddenly that Greg might confess his fears, his plans, his wants to Jason. It angered him Greg would abandon Stephanie.

Jason gave a brief nod, backed away. His boots clomped down the back steps. Stars appeared, darkness came on quickly and before long he could hear Jason clanking a wrench near the backhoe. He wondered how the kid could work in the dark like that. Maybe it was the difference between old eyes and young ones.

Greg awaited him in the small guest room next to the den, propped on a rocking chair next to a roll-out daybed, a plaid blanket covering his thighs and bloated belly. His hands trembled. Rusty didn't think disease had much to do with his appearance. He'd let himself go, denied himself nothing. His toes ached of gout, his physician recently uncovered hyperglycemia, his nerves demanded an output of energy that drew down most men in his condition to skin and bones. At first he'd tried herbs, nutritional remedies, later settled on donuts and Miller Lite, martini lunches, scotch and porterhouse steaks, cognac for an after-dinner mint. Beat the hell out of wheat grass and soy nuts, he informed Rusty. The downside was that it was tough to take a shit anymore and his hemorrhoids throbbed.

Greg asked after Angelique and laughed at Rusty's description of the lazy, not-too-bright boyfriend she'd adopted in Florida—hundreds such over the years—and he asked Rusty to tell the story of the World Famous Condor on Broadway and Columbus in San Francisco. First, Rusty told him, already sucked into the game, it wasn't the World Famous Condor until much later but a sex club nevertheless. Angelique went in with her male friend of the time, Rick or it was Gerald probably, and left Rusty, who was seven, in charge of his four-year-old brother. They watched sailors, prostitutes, business suits pass by on the crowded boulevard, the hawker outside the club trying to pull in customers, till a policeman approached and Rusty hustled away, his little brother in tow, fearing the officer would send them to an orphanage. On The Embarcadero he bought his brother a soda, too unsure of himself to eat a steamed crab. They got lost in returning and he had to ask strangers for the sex club. No one would talk to him until, driven to despair, he found a policeman, a different one, who goggled his eyes and asked what the hell was going on. My mom's there, he said and pretty soon they found Angelique screaming at the hawker, Gerald or whoever holding her back. Her arms swung wildly, she'd paid the son-of-a-bitch five bucks to watch her kids. It's okay, Rusty said and when she turned to see him she smacked his cheek so hard he fell to the pavement wailing. The policeman said hold on, he could take them away right now and she pretended to be placated. It was a job interview, she explained. She didn't want the sleazy job, she said. She said it was all Gerald's idea and he could go to hell. Rusty remembered the boyfriend rolling his eyes.

That one always made Greg laugh. Rusty relaxed for a moment. Greg chuckled, just as merrily as if he would live to hear the story again. His facial muscles couldn't grin but he could chuckle, even if it came out ghastly. That was the disease, Greg's booming laugh stifled by a stiff neck. He couldn't turn his head without rotating his entire torso, his cheeks creased and leathery, ashen as though a lifetime of sun had finally burned off the red-brown skin of his youth.

"What about Stephanie?" Rusty had married them a few years ago when they showed up unexpectedly to Alpine Bells after living together for twenty years.

"Change of subject?" he croaked. He sipped water. "Not now, okay?"

"Not now? When?"

"This from a divorced ... preacher ... condemns couples for a living." Greg enunciated every word as though having to command his tongue. "Getting tired again. It's not easy, Rusty ... maybe easier to let go because I've had it good." His body slumped into the rocking chair. Someone tapped at the door and they ignored it. Rusty checked his watch, more time gone by than he imagined. "Misery too," Greg murmured. "No regret."

Liar, Rusty thought. He read the spines on the bookshelf, recalled their conversation of a year ago. Camus: the only true philosophical query that remained was the question of suicide. Hedonism: to sustain an appropriate level of pleasure, while avoiding pain, for the longest possible period of time. Afterlife: a myth that quells good living. The Hemlock Society: here to help! Greg lay sideways on the daybed, his calves dangling awkwardly over the edge. He seemed to sleep, except for his shallow, steady breathing.

Walt was right. There could be no words of conflict. It might yet turn out to be a performance, Greg's bid for the kind of shortsighted immortality his artist friends thought was important, the kind where people quoted him and told stories about him until they met their own ends and everyone forgot. Everyone would remember September 10, 2001, until they didn't. Rusty's part had ended.

He helped his friend sit up, stuffed a pillow behind him. He told him he loved him, swallowed his friend in an embrace, let the tears run unchecked over his peppered beard.

"Don't make me cry," Greg whispered. He lifted white oxford sleeves to wipe his eyes. He bent at the waist to meet his sleeves. "This is strange ... haven't produced a tear for months now." In fact only a few drops blotted his sleeve while Rusty gushed and sniffled.

"I'm hogging all your time," he said. "All their time, I mean," Rusty threw his head in the direction of downstairs. They ignored another rap on the door. "I hope you'll ... ," but he left off the thought. He heard an engine rumbling in the yard. Jason, Greg said. He made Rusty tell another story, the one when Rusty and the little boys in the neighborhood walked over to the fairgrounds and sneaked in through the gaps in the old plank shacks that covered tractors and farm equipment to where the bulls were penned for the rodeo. One of them jumped onto the fence and hopped onto a bull and hopped to the other side, light as Peter Pan. The beast snorted and shook the metal pen. They dared Rusty, called him chicken. They had to hurry because someone might be coming. He jumped nearly sliding to the far side of the bull who reared and fell sideways crushing Rusty's knee against the fence. His friends pulled him clear and they had to run, Rusty gimping, biting his lip, trying not to cry. When he made it home with his crushed knee he asked Angelique to take him to the hospital and she said it served him right, going where he didn't belong. She sent him to bed and finally when he kept telling her it was broken took him to the hospital the next day. It was. He still gimped on it now and then when it hit the wrong angle.

There was an agreement among the six witnesses. Stephanie's friends explained everything ahead of time so there were no questions. Greg didn't want anyone to say a word. He wanted them in the room with him. Rusty didn't want to go in there any more than he wanted to witness a prisoner's execution but he honored his friend's wishes. A nurse, or someone who knew how to do an IV, had already hooked him up to a saline bag in the den. He sat in his barrel chair beneath a framed album cover of Woody Guthrie's *Dust Bowl Ballads*. Pretty Boy Floyd, the black lab he named after the Guthrie song, lay panting at his feet, his dull eyes rolling upward now and again. Looking only at his arm, Greg depressed a button for the painkiller. Now he had a minute or two to change his mind, or he could drift off to sleep and wake up tomorrow. To kill himself, he had to depress a second button for a lethal dose of Nembutal that would send him into a brief coma.

Rusty stood next to a portrait of the four of them at Zephyr Cove in front of the rickety cabin that belonged to Greg's paternal grandfather, the cabin they tore down to build a new one: he kept glancing at it, Stephanie and her sister Kate, Greg and Rusty, wondering how he could look at a photo that would be there always instead of his friend who would soon be gone. The psychiatrist named Farb swayed into his arm and muttered an apology, the only person in the room Rusty didn't know. They'd never met nor spoken a word together. Rusty didn't know why he was here. Stephanie kneeled beside Greg, appearing composed. He held the plastic lever in both hands, held it up in his lap as if to show his friends. He didn't look at any of them, instead shut his eyes. He leaned to whisper and whispered into Stephanie's ear. She touched his face and said something no one could hear, glanced over her shoulder since she'd violated the rules by speaking, an expression of panic on her face at this unrecoverable moment. Rusty moved as though to say his piece. The psychiatrist Farb put his open hand on Rusty's chest. Rusty wanted Greg to notice him though he had no intention to speak or to cry out as he sometimes later wished he had. He raised his hand to his chest and clasped Farb's hand. Tightly they held each other's hand.

Tyler Glenn and his wife, Dahlia, held each other. Larry Lufert, for the first time in anyone's recollection, stood mute. The others were downstairs or outside, by choice or by command.

Greg raised his head, his entire torso thrusting upward, pressing the button. Floyd let out a sudden yelp as if he'd been pricked and Stephanie grabbed the dog by the collar. Greg stared over the six of them, beyond them, focusing nowhere. He slumped into unconsciousness. Farb pronounced him in a coma and within minutes pronounced the time of death.

A false dawn lit the neighborhood as he stepped into the Vine Street bungalow in the same trance of mourning that had encompassed him since 11:58 p.m., the time of death. The rest was done quickly. Jason, who refused to be inside the house, had scooped out a gravesite at the back of the lot. The county needed a doctor's signature on the death certificate, then the body could be buried on private property within 24 hours. The pallbearers brought the pine coffin up the stairs and lugged it down. Dahlia Glenn offered the carpenter a blubbering compliment as they filed out into the chill air. Four men with shovels stood on a mound of mountain clay. Hurricane candles set round the gravesite flicked in the wind. Larry Lufert recited verse and someone played "Minstrel Boy" on the violin. He watched it all in silence, shocked when they asked him to say a blessing. The kerosene lamps turned to Rusty and he tasted ashes in his mouth.

Angelique wasn't home. He paced the upstairs hall and lumbered downstairs, tried to sit in the frayed green easy chair, picked up a book, tossed it onto the coffee table. He decided to take a walk in the cool dawn, recalled the weakest blessing he'd ever had to offer, unto dust, that was all he remembered himself saying, unto dust and surely we loved him, we'll miss him, and he ended up walking to Alpine Bells, the utter banality of what he'd had to say up there in Gold Hill haunting him alongside the grief. He unlocked the back door, smelled coffee, surprised to find anyone in so early, a newspaper spread on the table in the kitchenette. Quan Ping called him over. She huddled beside Stacy in front of the little television. Rusty couldn't understand what it was, a skyscraper in flames. Two towers burning, people jumping out of windows. As sunrise lit the break room, they watched a jet plane crash into the second building, the recording of it playing over and over. It had happened an hour ago. Then, panic creeping into the anchorman's voice, they watched one of the towers collapse, a volcanic plume rising where a skyscraper had been. Stacy curled her head into his chest, Quan Ping swore into the vacant air and Rusty said the only thing he could, that it would be okay, it would be okay, everything would be okay. ■

Interview with GARY T. CAGE

NR: What is your full title? How would you be addressed formally? Dr. Rev. Cage?

Cage: No, just my academic title, Dr. Cage. The religious movement I've been a part of eschews titles. So I would not have a title. In fact, the people in our church just refer to me by my first name. At most what you'll see is my name by the word "minister." But again, we really downplay the concept of clergy. We don't have a clergy/laity distinction in our religious fellowship. Sort of like Martin Luther; the things that he did dissolved that notion.

NR: Your church is called the "Foothills Church of Christ." How would describe it in general and what kind of congregation do you have? Just basic facts, bare numbers, things like that.

Cage: We're a small church. Our Sunday attendance is usually around 125; that counts all the children too. We built a building on the south end of town, off of Geiger Grade toward Virginia City, you can find it. Two major things I'm proud about with regard to that building: One was we made a decision as a group to build the building, and I was outvoted. I'm not a great fan of church buildings. I do see the good things that come out of them, but it's a big expense for the little bit of use that you usually get out of them, various activities and so forth—unless you have a school in it. And also there's sort of an attitude that people have, like a building is a holy place and God lives there, and I'm very much opposed to that kind of stuff. So the building's not holy; it's no more special than a warehouse. In the Bible, the word "church" refers to the people, and so the building does serve a good purpose to keep the rain and cold air out. It's functional. So I'm proud of the fact that I got outvoted, but we did it anyway. What that means is: I don't run the church. But I was out there, working on the building with everybody else. And that's the second thing I'm proud of: Except for those areas which we're required by the county to contract out, we built almost all of it with our own hands.

NR: How long did it take you to build it, and how many years have you been there?

Dr. Gary T. Cage is the pastor of the Foothills Church of Christ located in Reno, Nevada. The following interview was conducted in August 2009 by *The Nevada Review's* managing editor, Joe McCoy.

Cage: It took us 14 months to build it. And we finished on Thanksgiving weekend of 2005, and we moved into it. We've been in it coming up on 4 years.

NR: And before that you were over on Wedekind Rd. in north Reno, is that correct?

Cage: Yes. The building there was really too small, and we just didn't have enough land to expand the building.

NR: How many years have you been in Reno serving in this capacity?

Cage: As of September 2, 2009, I will have been here 30 years. And that is unusual for preachers of any stripe to be with the same church that long.

NR: Just to back up for a moment: You say there's no distinction between the clergy and the church members. There is no clergy then. It's the "priesthood of all believers."

Cage: That's it—the priesthood of all believers.

NR: But now you have some principal role. Would you describe that role as administrative?

Cage: I'm a hired technician. I have a knowledge of church work, church problems, church history, theological issues. If you're going to have a church, then one would think you have to have some people who give a lot of attention to that. And so there has developed over the centuries a tradition of training certain people, and they know a lot about church work. You hire them to be there to take care of a bit of it and to instruct others in how best it can be done.

NR: And this kind of work would include not just the maintenance and upkeep, but educational programs, arrangement of Sunday services, etc.

Cage: That's right. The preacher's work in our fellowship would be … we have some actual established or formal settings, Bible classes, assemblies, things like this. I'm expected to do a fair amount of teaching, so I'm teaching quite a bit during the week. And we have special classes that come up for special groups that I teach. We have readings in people's homes where I teach. Then there's the aspect of evangelism; if there's someone who would like to understand more about what the Christian faith is about, then I help with that. Then we come down to things like conflict resolution, counseling, marriage counseling, family counseling. Then matters that have to do with mission work, putting together mission programs, all the way down to even sometimes financial and administrative matters.

NR: One more question on this: Is there some sort of council or group that has some kind of administrative role that assists you?

Cage: In our congregation, we're sort of old-fashioned in certain aspects, and we encourage male leadership. And so once a month, the men of the congregation will meet and deal with various issues that need to be taken up as a church. A lot of delegation goes on, delegating these things out to other men, to committees, to groups of women. We have women on various committees. But, yes, so we have all kinds of committees that are set up to do various things in the church.

NR: If I understand correctly, the first church you served at was not in Reno but in Tennessee, your native state, and that's where you were born and raised?

Cage: True.

NR: Tell us a little bit about your early activities and education, perhaps starting with the years right before you came here, and your decision to move here.

Cage: Unlike Nevada, Tennessee has lots of small towns. You have almost as many different sizes of communities as you can imagine all the way up to large cities of 2 million. I was raised in a small town of about 12,000 people, about 30 miles outside the city of Nashville. What that means then is that my upbringing was half urban and half rural. It would not be unusual to see a tractor downtown in the town square. I was not raised on a farm; my wife was. But both of our families go way back; both of our families settled the state of Tennessee after participating in the Revolutionary War. Our families have a very rich history. So I was raised in a small town. My graduating class had, I think, about 180 people in the class. So fairly small, yet sizeable enough to have a lot of friends.

I did all the kind of things a person might imagine there. I was outside all the time playing baseball, riding bikes, camping out, fishing, that sort of thing. I went to the public schools and graduated from the local high school, and it was about as normal an existence for a young man as you could imagine in a rural setting in Tennessee. I would say that culturally we were somewhat behind the curve of the nation by about 10 years. For example, drugs became a problem in our small town in the mid-70s where I think they were a problem, say, on the West coast in the mid-60s.

I went to church. Now in the South of my youth, people went to church as part of the culture. They understood religion. Most people would have counted themselves as religious no matter how seldom they might go to a church service. They could probably name you the religious group they were a part of. People knew basics about the Bible, the life of Christ, and they talked about it a lot, and it informed their existence. So that was a big part of my life. My early church experience was very positive. It was enthusiastic and vigorous, and many youth groups there were really fine. There were preachers and members of the church who played a role in my life, who helped me to come to a point where I really felt that this was an important thing to do.

Then I left high school and went to a small, Christian college that was about the size of my high school. I think we had 734 students in the school enrolled the first year I attended in 1968. The name of that school was Freed Hardeman College in west Tennessee. Very conservative, somewhat fundamentalist. But our religious group, our religious heritage has always prized education, and I met people there with very fine credentials, accomplished in their fields. That's where I was first inspired towards philosophy and theology. That school did not have a complete, 4-year program, so I finished at another one called Harding College in Arkansas, and it was very much the same sort of character. But then I went to graduate school, which served as seminary even though our religious fellowship doesn't have a clergy or seminary *per se*, but it had advanced, terminal degrees that people could get. I took a normal Master's degree; I was there for 2 years. I was there when I got married my wife, Charlotte, with whom I had gone to high school. We married in 1972. I finished graduate school at Harding, but by then there had been built a fire in me to pursue philosophy. So I went on to Knoxville, Tennessee, where I went to the University of Tennessee and completed a PhD in philosophy. And I wanted to move away from religion when I did philosophy so I moved to the areas of epistemology and logic and wrote my dissertation on a question that had to do with a certain type of logic. While I was in Knoxville, though, I was introduced to some mission work in West Africa and that also played a part in my life, so that's pretty much my youth that gets me up to the time that I graduated.

NR: Did you serve as a minister then in Tennessee before you completed your studies?

Cage: Yes I did. I started out in a part-time fashion working with the church, the Arlington Church of Christ in Knoxville, Tennessee. They were very gracious and encouraged me in my studies. And then while I was working on my dissertation, I worked full-time with the church in Knoxville. I got my PhD there in Nashville, and at that time I made another move.

NR: Was that the point you went to Africa, or were you in Africa before that?

Cage: I had made a brief trip to Africa, and our plan was to go back to the country of Liberia, which would have to be one of the most primitive countries in Africa. We had made a mission trip there in 1975, that would be my wife and me, and then we were going back, but we had had two children by that time and there was a third one on the way. We have 3 sons, Zachary, Charlie, and Caleb, and we had some medical problems, and after consultation with some medical missionaries, we decided to forestall our trip to West Africa. And so, as this might be found humorous, I looked around for a place in the United States where I could go where I thought the mission field would be as challenging as Liberia, and I landed in Reno, Nevada.

NR: So you were casting about for different places, and that was one of the main criteria for your choice here. How did it work with the local congregation? Were they searching for a minister?

Cage: All of this is done through the grapevine. There's no central clearinghouse in our religious fellowship for this kind of thing. I had gone to college with a man from Reno, and he alerted me as to the possibility of my coming out and working. I flew out and met the people in this church, and we pretty much cut a deal. I came on out to work with them on September 2, 1979.

NR: Now the Foothills Church of Christ is part of the national Church of Christ movement or body. Is that the church of your youth too; you were raised in the Church of Christ?

Cage: Yes.

NR: And how would you characterize some of its basic perspectives and practices?

Cage: First of all let me say that anybody who'd go into philosophy is probably the kind of person who's going to question things a lot since that's the whole nature of philosophy. And I was always like that. I was always encouraged to ask questions to a good extent, but I am still in the religious heritage into which I was born; and it's because I think that the basic elements of this heritage are correct. Those basic elements are these: When our country was founded, there were a lot of people who were very excited about this new-found freedom. The freedom to study the Bible, the freedom to debate theological topics, and so forth, and they weren't controlled by the government or religious institutions. Our movement, which is sometimes called the "Stone-Campbell Movement," was very much an Enlightenment movement. What that means is that there was a very high appreciation and high regard for learning, education, the sciences, as well as advanced theology and philosophy. Many of the people who served early in this movement were freethinkers, and they got in trouble with a lot of groups.

America has a very strong influence from what we call "Calvinism." Even though Calvin himself probably had a fairly high regard for science and the intellect, his movement has not, and it's based on this idea of the "total depravity of man" and therefore the mind is tainted or corrupted by sin and so the product of the mind unaided by the Holy Spirit according to Calvinism is going to be tainted as well. If there's one thing that the founders of our movement shared was their rejection of Calvinism. The human mind is very fine; it is created by God. A non-Christian's mind can think just as well as Christian's mind; a non-Christian can understand the Bible just as well as a Christian. There's nothing inherently in the way. There was also this idea that we don't want to have to sign human creeds, but we want to leave the door open for a wide amount of disagreement.

Now as the years went by, this movement had its own problems, as they all do. Today it's made up of the Christian Church, the Disciples of Christ, and the Churches of Christ. I believe that you'll find in some of the churches, in some of the wings of this movement, that they've lost their way. They have become entrenched in certain doctrines, that you can't rethink them, you can't critique them, and I'm not happy with that. But I believe the church that I'm a part of here in Reno would represent more of this Enlightenment mentality of our founders.

NR: I assume that you wouldn't necessarily characterize it in a completely negative way, that is to say, your basic perspective is not a rejection of something, but I assume you would say it's an affirmation of the power of reason and the mind of man to know the truth and certain attendant powers like choice and judgment and things like that?

Cage: That's exactly what I would say. And so, yes, it wasn't so much a rejection as it was, as you said, an affirmation of the fact that all truth is God's truth—scientific truth is God's truth just as much as theological and even philosophical truth. The human mind has been made by God to apprehend this truth. We should get busy doing that. It's a very open-minded, critical look at theological issues and sometimes a willingness to debunk a traditional view.

NR: Can you give us an example of that?

Cage: Yes. Our movement started out to be as inclusive as we possibly could. But one of the things we repeatedly ran into back in the early

1800s was the idea that man is free to accept or reject God's plan. What that means is that any human being can come upon the Gospel, can understand it, and then stand in a position either to choose it or not choose it. He chooses it by being baptized; baptism became a big issue our fellowship, because it was this free embrace of God's program. Now 200 years ago that was not a widely accepted point of view. In a nutshell, Calvinism would say to varying degrees that God sorts through human beings and more or less chooses those whose hearts He will open up and those He won't, and that without that, a person is not able to understand the Gospel plan and accept it. Therefore, baptism became an afterthought; it was something you did after God saved you. God found you and saved you. And also this whole idea of a religious experience that was very big during the Second Great Awakening in America, this idea that God would do something to you, salvation would happen to you. This is one of those traditional views we debunked. Also, in the Stone-Campbell Movement, Barton Stone himself rejected the doctrine of the Trinity though Campbell accepted it. And these two men found that okay and could accept each other and move on. But the Trinity would be regarded by many as a foundational tradition. So early on our movement raised for reconsideration many of these views that were at that time considered established.

NR: So then just to look at this from an individual perspective, it must be then that, prior to joining your congregation, an individual is going to have to engage in a period of study and reflection about these things. I would take your implication to be that they can't just walk off the street and become baptized.

Cage: That's exactly right. Though there's some variety amongst the Churches of Christ, we actually dispensed with the so-called "altar call" many years ago where at the end of the sermon there would be an invitation to come forward and be baptized. We make a much more general invitation to people that, if you're interested in knowing more, we're here to serve you individually. But we're very strong on the idea that a person's basic questions need to get answered before they can accept the faith. So we spend time, sometimes many months in studying the Bible with people, before they are baptized.

NR: And does that continue in the life of the congregation, this ongoing study of the Bible and historical sources?

Cage: Our movement is very study-oriented, and sometimes people don't like that and have seen us as a little too academic, with too little emotion. Although I do believe there needs to be a balance between the two, I think, if anything in America today, Christians probably need to be a little more academic. They need to know more and study more. Going back to this idea of the pursuit of the truth, I found my religious heritage had somewhat fossilized in the South, and one of the reasons that I left and came to a free-wheeling state like Nevada was the hope that I could find a fellowship where there would be this openness to reconsidering every point of view and discussing it without people getting scared and upset and even hostile towards each other.

NR: Are you saying then you believe you've actually had that experience in Nevada and that there is a kind of openness to some of these questions?

Cage: It hasn't come easy. But I sometimes tell people that the Foothills Church of Christ is a libertarian church. By that I mean we have a core—and every church would have to have a core—we have a core, but we make that core as small as we believe we can get by with and then allow people a wide range of different of points of view outside that core. And even the core itself can be reevaluated from time to time. There's no proposition that we as a group believe is not open to reconsideration and possible revision.

NR: One of the things I'm curious about is the difference in the religious sensibilities of the people you were born and raised among and the sensibilities of people like Nevadans—or the absence of religious sensibilities. My understanding has been, and you can correct me on this if I'm wrong, that Nevada is one of the least religious states in terms of churches per square mile, number of regular attendees per capita, etc. and I imagine Tennessee is quite high on the list in that regard.

Cage: You're exactly right. Nevada is number 50. Whatever standard you use when you judge all 50 states, Nevada is number 50. It's a very secular state. In fact, the whole northwestern United States is very secular—northern California, northern Nevada, Idaho, Oregon, that area, very secular. And that's been a good thing, because it's allowed us an opportunity to start fresh.

Now you're right about those sensitivities. We have had people from various religious backgrounds be a part of our church for a period of time and just find it intolerable, because they believe that certain things just need to be nailed down and defended. I remember one time a fellow left our fellowship, and he said, "I'm leaving because when I come to church I don't want my views to be challenged." Well, I understand that, because a lot of churches don't challenge views; they pretty much dispense your views and then proceed to defend them. On the other hand, we have a lot of people who come from various backgrounds, secular, even atheistic, backgrounds and other church backgrounds, who have very much welcomed an opportunity to raise questions and to discuss them openly and be allowed to hold various viewpoints. So, yes, I believe we've been able to put that together.

NR: How would you compare the two states and populations in terms of sensitivity to denomination? You mentioned earlier that back in Tennessee a person would not only say he was a Christian, but he could tell you the name of that church. I would imagine that in Nevada it's much more muted and that denomination is not quite as big a deal out here.

Cage: The fact of the matter is that the American culture has changed dramatically in the 30 years in which I've been out here. One of the major changes in America is that denominational tags mean far less than they ever have in the past. Now in the state of Tennessee, for example, you would still find that means more to more people than in the state of Nevada. One of things you find here is that you've got lifestyle issues. People aren't as concerned with the fine-tuning of doctrine as much as they are with what difference this is going to make to their lives.

NR: Certainly given the culture and the economic profile, the way Nevada works in terms of its industry, that must make a difference in terms of the people you encounter and the kinds of issues, difficulties, or problems that they bring when you encounter them.

Cage: I should think that every minister or religious leader in this town would say that Nevada has a lot of hurting people, and you spend a lot of your time with substance abuse problems, marriage problems, psychological problems that come out of sin, like guilt and loneliness and depression. Yes, that's going to be a little larger here than in most places.

NR: In some ways, then, you would view this lack of sensitivity to denomination and certain doctrinal things as a silver lining; it's an opportunity for you to talk to people who might not have spoken to you otherwise.

Cage: That's right. When a person says, well I am a Dutch Reformed, or something like that, they're saying, in so many ways, this is what I believe. Now that's fine as long as they're willing to critique that, and that goes for me too. But as a rule, people aren't. They're saying that's a settled fact. However, there's a downside when you have an atmosphere where traditional denominational distinctions are not taken so seriously, you'll find that people aren't as concerned about the truth as much either. So it's a trade-off, and I think a lot of people here would maybe choose Rastafarianism if it got them through the night. So you have to deal with that side of it as well. Somehow you have to balance a sincere pursuit of the truth with the impact of this pursuit on a person's daily life.

NR: You mentioned this word "truth" and as you already mentioned you've had training in philosophy and you're a professor of philosophy here in Reno, at the university. Do you think that that concern with truth was something you brought to your religion or that it was already there and philosophy complemented it?

Cage: Actually, I think the latter. I think that's one of the differences about our religious heritage was that this attitude about truth was out there. Now I'm not saying that we have always managed to keep that attitude. I think one of the problems is fear. When a person opens up and says I want to go pursue the truth and see where it lands, that's scary, it's frightening. I might find out that something I believed, I don't believe anymore and that might change my life. So everybody has that problem, and there's an element of bravery that goes with pursuing the truth. But our fellowship started out with this open-minded pursuit of the truth: Let's go see what the texts of the Bible really says, let's do philosophy, let's do an evidential critique of the Christian faith.

NR: Do your parishioners find this philosophical approach to religion and religious questions surprising or unexpected in other ways? Is that unusual or atypical approach?

Cage: It is unusual, and I've resisted that conclusion for some time. But I believe it's unusual. Certainly there are other churches out there that practice that; I'm sure that's true. But it is unusual. Now people who come amongst us and stay, usually stay for that reason, that they find their minds stimulated by looking at other possibilities.

NR: Your church has a website in addition to its main website at www.foothillschurchofchrist.com. The other one is www.evidencestudy.com, and that provides quite a lot of early Christian documents, archeological data, and other information related to early Christianity. What is the purpose of this website and the making available of this data?

Cage: I believe that for the first 300 years in the history of the Christian faith there was one basic approach to proselytization and that was a presentation of evidence. It would be things like: Here are some people who say they saw the resurrected Jesus; here is a succession of people who go back to the early Apostles; here are some of our early documents; here are non-Christians who report things about the Jesus movement, and this sort of thing. And then there's a lot of argument amongst and against even the detractors of religion in these first 200 or 300 years. For example, detractors like Celsus who would raise possible contradictions with some of the *New Testament* writings. This was around A.D. 165 or 170. We find that there were early writers, like Tertullian and Origen, who wrote against these detractors and gave answers. So it was an culture which invited disputation, a forensic sort of atmosphere in which Christianity was promoted. Now I'm not going to say that there weren't other things, like the lifestyle of these Christians and their community, that people found attractive and the servanthood of these people. I think that always plays a role. But I think the early Christians would have said that nothing about our lives really matters if we cannot give you a plausible case for the truth of Christianity based on primarily the resurrection of the man, Jesus.

NR: There are traditional arguments for God's existence; you have arguments like the ontological argument, the cosmological argument, the teleological argument, things like that. But is it actually your view that in some sense the resurrection of Jesus can be proven? That it can be demonstrated?

Cage: Demonstrated, yes. The word "proven" carries with it some ideas sometimes that I wouldn't want to go with. The fact of the matter is that there's nothing even in the sciences that's absolutely proven. All you have to do is hang around for a while and watch the most recent scientific view change. However, there are points of view about historical matters, scientific matters, and so forth that are very well established—so well-established that a person who has looked at the evidence should rationally conclude that such-and-such occurred. And that's exactly what I'm saying about the resurrection of Jesus, that there is a very strong, rational argument. And I can't think of an alternative analysis of the evidence that is more plausible than the one that Jesus really did rise from the dead.

NR: Out of curiosity, what are some alternative explanations that you encounter and deal with in this sort of study?

Cage: The most popular, current alternative view to the resurrection among people who have looked at the evidence—and the alternatives change from century to century—I don't mean the popular ones, but among people who have looked at the evidence—is that what we have here is some sort of mass hysteria, that there was this desire for Jesus to live on and it was so strong that people began to believe that maybe Jesus had risen. But it was an emotional delusion.

The next alternative that has sometimes played into it that is a little less strongly held is that it grew up in a legendary fashion over a period of time. This would be, I believe, the basis of these books, like

The Davinci Code and *Holy Blood, Holy Grail*. You have to have a lot of time though to elapse for this legend to grow up.

The least likely one, by all serious students of the evidence, is that it was a conspiracy. I don't know any serious historians who believe that the resurrection story was the result of a conspiracy.

NR: But why not? In our own time we do see religions being generated before our very eyes. A professor of mine used to say, quite seriously, that there's a new religion created in California every day. Why can't we say that the early Christian movement was a similar phenomenon?

Cage: Well, there are several reasons for it. Probably the most dramatic reason, and I'm not ashamed to bring up this well-worn defense, is that this was costing people their lives. Secondly, the teaching of the resurrection of Jesus came around so early that we can easily establish it in the 50s of the 1st Century A.D., and there are some good clues that it was going around in the 40s, that certainly there were plenty of people around who would be able to contradict it and say, "No, that's not what our movement was about. Who came up with such a hare-brained notion, and you're going to get us all killed." That was a big thing. Another thing is: What was in it for the perpetrators of this conspiracy? Was it money? Was it fame? Was it ambition? It certainly didn't seem that it had any of these things to offer. Now in the United States where a person can come up with a hare-brained notion and make a few million dollars out of it, you can sort of see where it might come from. But there's no indication that that was the case. So you put all that together and other aspects as well, and these alternative explanations just do not seem very likely ... and not to mention that conspiracies are notoriously difficult to pull off.

NR: I suppose they're especially difficult to pull off if a lot of the evidence you're citing is public, the claims to public appearances.

Cage: Yes, which they made.

NR: What would you say to somebody who came to you perfectly willing to accept Jesus as a great teacher, a very moral person, but not divine and not divinely appointed, but a wise man, like a Buddha or a sage of some sort like that? What would be so wrong about believing that?

Cage: Well, if you go back to our early sources, many aspects of the Christian faith are based on this the resurrected Jesus, that he was more than a teacher, and he got this from God and that he had demonstrated the truth of this by his resurrection. One of the main issues here is that his death on the cross is an atonement for sin, and why would anybody believe that another crucified Jew, that his death was an atonement for sin? Well, the reason put forward is that God raised him from the dead. And lastly I'd mention that the whole thing about Christianity is that it's a spiritual kingdom. Jesus doesn't sit on a throne in Palestine, but he sits on a throne in Heaven, and it's a spiritual kingdom. That spiritual aspect of Christianity was based on the resurrection of Jesus. That changed everything. It would take me far too long to explain that now, but I'll say it that simply.

So you ask, what would be so wrong? Well, I think it's mistaken—let's use that word—that the person would be mistaken. They just don't see this issue in its fullness. Now if that's all a person knows and that's the best they understand, then that's the best they can do.

NR: This philosophical and evidence-based approach, which would include the discernment and pursuit of the truth ... are you also saying this is characteristic of the early Christians? Did they argue in this fashion?

Cage: They absolutely did. I don't find any of the emotionalistic aspects amongst the surviving materials that we have from the early Christians. They were making the case that this really happened: Jesus rose from the dead and that that had rocked their world, and that they were prepared to defend it. So they made this rational argument, a rational explanation. I do personally believe that they worked miracles too and that was an added, rational demonstration. Sometimes people call miracles "irrational," and I don't understand that. I can't imagine anything more rational than a person working miracles.

NR: Why would you say that? Somebody might deny that, because a miracle seems by definition to be a violation of the laws of nature, or a suspension of those laws, and therefore, it would have to be a *per se* irrational event.

Cage: That's if you define "irrational" as "anything that violates a law." But if, for example, a governing authority were to overrule an existing law in our country for a particular reason, we wouldn't say necessarily that was irrational. We'd understand why it happened. So the overruling of a natural law would be about the clearest and most rational demonstration of the existence of a god as anything I could imagine.

NR: Let me ask you this: This philosophical and evidence-based approach to religion, what room does it allow for faith? I guess my question really is: What is "faith" in your view? Or is there no such thing, and it's all rational demonstration?

Cage: I pretty much differ with the mainline view of faith in American Christianity. The mainline view is that faith is a gift that God gives you, that one accepts the Gospel without evidence, or even worse, that one accepts it in spite of contravening evidence. That's the worst I can imagine. But the biblical view of faith is that there are two parts to it: One is coming to the rational conclusion that the story is true, and then the second part is entrusting yourself to it. If you were on a high-wire and you were walking across this high-wire and you were pushing a wheelbarrow across that high-wire, I might be amazed that you were able to do that. And you might say to me, "Gary, do you believe that I can get to the other side pushing this wheelbarrow across this high-wire?", and I might say, "Well, I think maybe you can; you look pretty amazing." Then at that point you might say, "OK then, get in the wheelbarrow." And that's what I think faith is: You have very strong reasons for believing something is true, but there is that additional step where you get in, you commit to it. That's an aspect I think is sometimes overlooked. But even there it's not certain. I would not tell you that I'm certain that Christianity's true, but it seems like it most likely is.

NR: That's what I was going to ask you. You said a moment ago that no factual question can be proved 100%, like a mathematical theorem or something. So could you in theory imagine circumstances under which you would come to the conclusion that this story doesn't make sense to you anymore?

Cage: Sure.

NR: In that vein then: In your ministry, when you present this approach and you're going through these kinds of evidence studies, how would you characterize the roadblocks, the inhibitions, the objections and difficulties people have with it? Would you say they're primary theoretical? Or would you primarily say it's the hesitancy to place themselves in the wheelbarrow, a kind of moral or practical inhibition? Or is it a combination of both?

Cage: You can find almost anything out there. I have met people in Nevada who simply had never thought about God. The thought had never occurred to them any more than joining a basket weaving club. It had just never occurred to them. So with these people then it's just a matter of setting forth the case and then you see what they do with it.

For most people though, you hit the nail right on the head; there's this moral issue. Dinesh D'Souza says in his book, *What's So Great About Christianity?*, that what lies at the base of most skepticism and resistance to Christianity is sexual license. We want to be free sexually; we want to do whatever we wish. I think he's got his finger on part of the truth there. If you don't want to accept something, you can find all kinds of reasons not to. That's that freedom thing. There's also the desire not to be inconvenienced; we don't want to be inconvenienced with servanthood, other people's lives, the discipline of living a Christian life. We don't want to make changes. And so, yes, that can get in the way. In my 35 years of preaching and mission work, I'm prepared to say that in most cases, that's the underlying problem.

NR: But what would you say to somebody? I mean, it does seem to be clear that if they were going to accept this fellowship in your church or a church like yours, they're going to have to alter their life in some ways, and it's going to upset and unbalance a lot of things. Would you discuss these changes in terms of some greater pay-off for them?

Cage: I absolutely would. A person should always do what is best for himself. Now we define that in our culture as selfish, and I don't think that's true. A person should always do what is best for himself. I am a follower of Jesus of Nazareth, because I want to be with God eternally, and it just turns out, though, one of the really great things about the Christian faith, that whatever is best for me turns out to be best for everybody else too. In other words: Never would my doing the right thing be the wrong thing for someone else.

NR: But then don't you come back to this other side of the question, because how do you know what the right thing is? And the Christian claim is a pretty large claim, and it's not easy just to sign off on that in one fell swoop.

Cage: I think that's why God has so fixed this world where people run into, let us say, opportunities. A person has problems with substances, a person loses a loved one, a person suffers a divorce, financial ruin, things like that, and they're hurting really bad. It's those moments of clarity that offer people, I think, an opportunity to want to seek the truth of Christianity. I honestly think a person has to want to seek the truth, they have to want it even if this truth is going to be difficult.

NR: You just described these cases of pretty profound pain as "opportunities." Is your view that there is genuine pain in the world?

Cage: Pain is not inherently evil, any more than pleasure is inherently good. With a moment's reflection you can see in your life that pain has served you well on some occasions, and pleasure has not served you well on some occasions. So what is God after? God is after us seeing the truth. He wants us to get it. He wants us to see that an eternal relationship with Him is far more important than anything else. And yes, all suffering plays a role in that.

One of the things I always come to when I think of terrible pain—and I have seen extraordinary pain in the lives of so many people in 35 years of working in the ministry—one of the conclusions is that that's just exactly how serious this whole matter is. You would not allow terrible pain to occur in a person's life in order to teach them how to be a better baseball player. Some pain, sure, but not the terrible things we often see. Why would God then do that? I believe the answer is that our learning to deal with sin and our coming to know God and having an eternal relationship is truly worth all the depth of pain we see in this world.

NR: Is this pain a necessary precondition somehow for one choosing to accept God's plan?

Cage: I really don't see how, for most people, that you can get it without some degree of pain.

NR: I wonder if we can just rephrase this problem of pain and suffering in the following way: Why does it have to be so intense and deep? Why couldn't God have sort of narrowed the channels or reduced the scope of the world so that we would just have less occasion to suffer? Allow us to make some decisions without as many sharp edges and occasions to fall off in these terrible kinds of suffering and viciousness that we see every day?

Cage: Of course that question comes from a certain perspective; it comes from ours. You will therefore probably find what I'm going to say here a strange thing, but if the worst things that ever happened to human beings were hangnails and bad hair days, we would wonder how God could allow hangnails and bad hair days. Now let's go to the other extreme. God could have created a world where we were in constant, conscious pain every second of every day for long, long lives—so painful that we hardly have the clarity of mind to even consider our predicament. We're not even in the middle between those two. Even in the parts of the world where people live in poverty, to us it looks pretty bad, but even there a lot of these people have a tolerable life. Now there certainly are people who don't. And so what I'm saying is that I think God has measured out just the amount of pain we need, and we'll never agree with Him on that. We'll always think it's too much.

NR: We've been talking about this very rational, evidence-based approach. At the heart of this—these basic choices people make, the actual climbing into the wheelbarrow—aren't there also emotional elements to that? Is there some kind of immediate experience of God in those occasions? How would you characterize it?

Cage: I confess that I don't know exactly how active God might actually be in this world. It is possible that God has set up the parameters of the way this world works, and He knows us and nature so well that He knows that, as we live life, we're going to come to come to these opportunities. I tend to think that sometimes even then God does put His hand into the state of affairs to create an emotional circumstance that will generate a desire to look at the truth. So in answer to your question, I would say there's got to be a balance. I would not want to live an emotionless life, and I certainly don't want to live an irrational life. I think both of them are important.

I sometimes use this example: If I came to you today and I said, "I have a top of the line flamethrower and I'm willing to sell it to you today. It's brand-new. It's ready to go. It's fully operable, and I'd like to sell it to you for 75% off." Now that's a deal, that's a bargain, but only if you feel the need for a flamethrower. Otherwise, it doesn't move you at all. Somehow, I think, God has built this world where we come to these places where we're moved, where we have an opportunity to be moved, to see the need, to feel the purpose of it all. But then we have to go to the other side: If there's no good reason to believe that the Gospel is true, then why should we accept that? So I think you have to feel the need, but then also to see it as true.

NR: So then you would say then in your ministry that there is this desire and hunger for this relationship with God, but would you also say there is this desire for a rational approach to God? Do you see that?

Cage: I don't find that as much as I used to. I think that our culture is going through an irrational phase. You even have the name, "the postmodern predicament." However, those relativistic moods are always short-lived, and I'm beginning to see what I think is a snap-back in our culture, and people want something of substance. They'd like to know that there's something really there. They're tired of the relativism; it really makes you quite crazy. So they're looking for something with substance. So, yes, both of those things are going on: People are living in this fragmented world of ours, and they're suffering the neurosis that comes from that. They're looking for something that has some substance in it upon which they can place their feet. So they are looking for that rational aspect too.

NR: I wonder if you encounter anything of that sort in your teaching. I assume that you don't evangelize in your philosophy classes, but you must touch on similar topics, big picture issues that come up, and I wonder if, in purely philosophical contexts, you encounter this generally skeptical or cynical stance.

Cage: I think "cynicism" is the word, and in my college classes, these young people are very untrusting. And why should they be trusting? Just about everything in their lives has broken down. So they're hurting; they're pessimistic. Of course, you're right: When I teach a philosophy class, I teach a philosophy class, but one cannot help see from semester to semester this deterioration of optimism, and even other professors who I know are not Christians see the same thing and often speak of it.

NR: And does this impact how educable and how open these students are to questions of this sort?

Cage: You do see that. I think there is a hunger for looking at all kinds of alternatives out there. Yes, there is sort of an openness, that's a good thing that's come out of all of this. There's sort of a willingness to look at other options, other alternatives. If there's one thing that I think can be said of our young people in American culture right now is that they're tired of a lot of the traditional alternatives and that includes a lot of traditional Christianity, and they're looking at other possibilities.

NR: Do you find that there's a kind of rhetorical problem just sort of bringing up the name "Jesus" or using a word like "church" or "sin," or words like that? Does that set off alarms bells in people? Do they rankle at that, do they have negative reactions to that kind of thing quite apart from the content?

Cage: Only in a minority of the students. Fortunately in Nevada, we still have something of a traditional college atmosphere where there's an openness to considering all possibilities out there and critiquing. That is allowed in our schools here, and that's a good thing. There are students who will sneer at Christianity, but then they'll sneer at religion, but they'll also sneer at authority. They'll sneer at a lot of things. So you're always going to have some of that, but actually I've found students willing to discuss Islam, Buddhism, Christianity, all of these fairly open-handedly.

NR: Do you see any trends as to where this generation is inclining? You say they're looking for other, non-traditional ways; where do you see it heading?

Cage: The pundits say that the 21st Century is going to be the most religious century in the history of the United States, but it won't be Christianity. They're probably right; the United States is probably going the way of Europe. That would be my guess; however, you know this country has bucked quite a few trends in the past, and one can never tell.

NR: Are you saying that Islam will become the predominant religion in America? The demographics in Europe make it seem like that's fairly certain.

Cage: What I see is sort of a New-Age sort of thing, which, in my opinion is an Americanized version of Hinduism and Taoism, that there will be this New-Age mentality—people will call themselves "spiritual" if they enjoy a walk in the woods. Something like that. So that's where I see people going. Now, you never know, if there were some severe situations, drastic situations in our country where our survival was threatened, I wouldn't be surprised if there'd be a shift to some of our traditional roots.

NR: With this fraying of our institutions and this cynicism, I could well imagine some sort of spiritual or religion renaissance, but one that's not necessarily a very rational one. It might be highly unsalutary and maybe even dangerous.

Cage: You know, Salman Rushdie once compared Islamic fundamentalism to Christian fundamentalism, and I see some of those comparisons as being real. So, yes, you could find that. There are no utopias, and in the fog of war, you never know how things are going to turn out. And so some people would react emotionally, some more rationally.

NR: Sometimes people connect this modern "openness" to modern skepticism. But you seem to have come back to the "traditional alternative." Is that fair to say?

Cage: One might say that with this open-minded pursuit of the truth—"It seems, Gary, that you still sort of landed with traditional Christianity." To that I would have to respond, "Yes and no." I do believe that it's a historical fact that Jesus was raised from the dead just as it is a historical fact that Caesar crossed the Rubicon. I believe that the God of Abraham, Isaac, and Jacob really exists. However, this reconsideration of traditional Christian doctrine has led me to a lot of different places. Not to go down the list, that would be too lengthy. Probably one of the most notable ones is one that's been very troubling in the history of Christianity, and it has to do with the so-called second coming of Christ. Skeptics and detractors of Christianity have been quite right to point out that Jesus promised that he would come back in the lifetimes of his disciples, those standing there with him, and apparently he did not. That's been a big problem. One of the things I've come to see in my study is that all of the "end times" language that we find in the *New Testament* is really a reference to the destruction of Jerusalem that occurred in A.D. 70 in the lifetimes of Jesus' apostles and disciples. And therefore what he said was correct; it was just to be understood figuratively, and that those figures were actually taken from the *Old Testament.* So what I'm trying to say is that in numerous areas I've actually landed in a spot different than a lot of Christians. I haven't landed on those spots because I like them more; I've landed on those spots because I believe they're more likely true than the traditional interpretation.

NR: So to clarify: You would say that most Protestant denominations, Catholic and Orthodox churches probably do accept this "end times, dissolution-of-the-world" interpretation of the Bible? You regard it as an actual prophecy about an actual event, but it occurred in A.D. 70?

Cage: Yes.

NR: Why was A.D. 70 and the destruction of the Temple so important? Essentially what you're saying is that there's a whole book of the *New Testament*, the book of *Revelation* or *Apocalypse*, written to describe this event and numerous references throughout the *New Testament*—why was that so earth-shattering, so to speak?

Cage: Because it was the end of the Jewish religious economy. I believe that that's what the early Christians saw themselves as being, this displacement or extension, of the Jewish religious economy. Not that Jews were cut off from it. Jews could join and they did, Paul and Peter and those people being outstanding examples of such. But God had started a new program; it's a spiritual program as opposed to a physical one. So Jerusalem had to go, the Temple had to go, these physical trappings had to go in order for people to stop clinging to them and then to open the door for this spiritual movement.

NR: Would you describe other institutional, historically established Christian churches as beset with similar "physical trappings"?

Cage: We're bent that way; it's the way our spade is turned. We like physical trappings. And, yes, people look at the clergy, they look at rituals, they look at church buildings as holy. I believe that's a mistake.

NR: I'm not trying to be mischievous in asking this—and you've said previously that you don't consider yourself the authority of your church, that you're working alongside the other people in your fellowship—but is it the case that some of your co-religionists, your fellow parishioners are kind of disappointed in this view of the "end times"? It's awfully exciting to talk about the end of the world and you're kind of saying, well, it's just not really that central of a feature.

Cage: In politics and in literature and in religion, there is the lure of sensationalism. Sometimes the truth is not immediately sensational. I tend to find the truth sensational just because it's the truth. I get really excited about that when I think I might have found something that opens up vistas to understanding more truth. But, yes, it is the case that for most people that's disappointing. We live in a culture though where we're used to having more. We want more, and therefore, we're disappointed when that's all there is to it. We see this unfortunately in marriages, and we see this with people's jobs, and they say, "Is that all there is to it"? And it's at that point that people often do some pretty crazy things. So, yes, some of my views are not sensational, and because of that, that's a little bit of a problem.

NR: I was just listening to an interview before this by a British social commentator, Theodore Dalrymple, and he was really talking about the licit drug culture in the Western world, but it also blurred over into the illicit use of drugs as well. One of the things he said about both cases—the abuse of both legal and illegal drugs he thought was mainly a fight against spiritual malaise and boredom. People are just not excited about life and that's what they do as a kind of *ersatz* fulfillment.

Cage: Boredom is a luxury that pampered people can afford. And we have in our affluent society the luxury of being bored.

NR: Sloth is one of the seven deadly sins, is it not?

Cage: I don't know.

NR: I used to know these things back in my catechism days.

Cage: I might throw this one out too. I think that it certainly is true that Christians have given atheism, agnosticism, and skepticism plenty of fodder over the centuries. Not only their just out-and-out wicked behavior that certainly works against us; their mistreatment of people other than Christian groups has certainly worked against them. I think in modern America this whole issue of faith as a mystical endowment that is outside the parameters of investigation has really put Christianity in the arena of mental illness.

NR: Really what you're saying is that many, many Christians and most atheists share that same view of faith.

Cage: Yes, as an irrational thing, and people are right when they say, I choose not to accept irrationality. A lot of American Christianity has been just that. Also, I would argue that a lot of Christian groups have exacerbated the tension by trying to weave too much Christianity into the government, in the legislation, they're actually going to use the power of government—which is always force, it's always a gun—ultimately to force people to behave. I'm one of those Christians with no desire to force other people to behave along the lines that I would like to see them go. I think we all understand that my freedoms need not interrupt your freedoms, but that's just as far as I'm concerned to go.

NR: Do you see that particular phenomenon as important in America today? It does seem for a pretty solid century, in terms of the relation between religion and politics, there has been an ever-increasing disentanglement of the two.

Cage: Well, I think that's true. The entanglement began in the early 19th Century, and in the 19th Century we wove a lot of Christianity into our legislation. That was a mistake. What we need is to go back to Jeffersonian republicanism where the idea there is that people have the freedom to be religious or not; that whatever kind of religion they decide on that they should be as free as we can possibly allow them to be. A case in point along that line would be: I have no desire to legislate marriage; I'd like to de-politicize it as something not in the domain of government anymore. Individuals can choose to be married as they see fit, and churches can choose to regard marriage as they see fit.

NR: So you don't see any compelling state reason to protect or underwrite the institution of marriage?

Cage: I do not. I'm not a big believer in the government's ability to do much good. It can serve a purpose to constrain other people in certain areas, but it really doesn't solve any problems. It's more of a negative force than it is a positive force. So I have no desire to use the power of the government to promote Christian values. Now I personally believe and personally suspect that, if we would allow people to be free, more people would be put into a position where they could see the truth of Christianity.

NR: Well, let me try to push you on this a little bit more: Surely you would grant that, at some point, the state does have a compelling reason to constrain or force or act as a barrier separating one person from another, in the case of violent attacks and things like this?

Cage: Only on the most minimal basis and that is when your freedom gets in the way of my freedom. I believe that was our Founding Fathers' majority opinion.

NR: So is freedom then a value? Is it a good?

Cage: I think that it is a good, but that's irrelevant. Freedom is the only rational approach. What's the alternative to allowing people to pursue their own good? When Jefferson wrote "the pursuit of happiness," the concept of happiness for him was different than it is in America. Happiness for Jefferson was pursuit of good, and I think that you ought to be able to pursue what you think is good as much as you wish, and I should be able to pursue what I think is good even if it's different from your concept as much as I wish—the only limit on that being when my pursuit of the good begins to get in the way of your pursuit of the good. And so there would have to be some restraints set up to moderate our individual pursuits of the good. What I'm against is any group, including Christians, deciding for the rest of us what's good.

NR: Let me approach it this way: Jefferson was an advocate of free public education, and one of the basic Enlightenment doctrines is that a system of free, public education is necessary, because we do need an educated citizenry for it to be able to govern itself. Now that seems to me to imply several things, one of those things being that free public education is, of course, not free; it requires a tax base and tax collection. By virtue of this public good being instituted in the form of schools, we're going to have to consent and cede certain natural liberties. Is that not true? We're going to have to consent to be taxed, and there will be certain burdens on parents to place their kids in these schools, and so there would be a constriction of natural liberty.

Cage: Jefferson also had slaves ...

NR: That's right.

Cage: Jefferson made mistakes.

NR: Of course, the difference with Jefferson is that—whether you think he was ultimately consistent or a hypocrite—he actually opposed the institution of slavery, where he actually proposed and advocated for a public system of education. You think he was flat wrong on that.

Cage: He was wrong. He wasn't perfect; he was great. But he was wrong about that. Most errors in a culture start out as a good idea. We see a need, we want to address that need, it seems like the right thing to do. But somewhere down the line, there are those unintended consequences. I believe that small communities and individuals working in voluntary concert can do far more good in this world than any other way. I'm for everyone who wants an education to have the freedom to pursue it. We often think that without the government providing things, that people won't get those things. I'm just not convinced.

NR: Do you see a historical epoch or a geographical region that more or less corresponds to this idea, as you said, this community freely working in concert with each other without this superimposed regulation from the government?

Cage: Well, yes, I think the early Republic before the Civil War there was an actual self-conscious awareness of just these very concepts. I certainly don't believe they pulled it off perfectly, and no one ever will, but they understood that concept. And there are places out west of the

Mississippi, a place like Nevada, where you still find the vestiges of it, though those vestiges are rapidly disappearing.

NR: I was recently told by a friend of mine that Southerners don't necessarily like Yankees, but Westerners aren't Yankees, and there's a certain honorific status Westerners have because they're still free.

Cage: Yes.

NR: Dr. Cage, thank you for your time. ■

Book Reviews

Glotfelty, Cheryll (ed.). *Literary Nevada: Writings from the Silver State*. Reno: University of Nevada Press, 2008. 896 pages, $60.00/$29.95—Nevada seems made for literature. In few places can the ephemeral fortunes and desires of man be so vividly contrasted with the seeming stability and silence of the surrounding landscape. Yet few can list more than a couple of authors who have written about the Silver State and its people.

Cheryll Glotfelty has given a wonderful gift to Nevadans and to anyone interested in Nevada's culture and history, both natural and human, in putting together the first comprehensive anthology of Nevada literature: *Literary Nevada: Writings from the Silver State*. This truly wide-ranging anthology contains multiple genres, admirable ethnic and gender diversity, and broad historical range—from Native American stories to newly published works. The collection contains both Nevada writers and outsiders writing about their perception of Nevada. The qualifying attribute seems to be that each literary work allows the reader to understand some aspect of Nevada as it exists and as it is experienced. Both well-known authors, such as Mark Twain, Sarah Winnemucca, John Muir, and Walter Van Tilburg Clark, as well as new voices, such as Jeffery Chisum, Aliki Barnstone, and Verita Black Prothro, are included. Each individual selection has been given a brief, informative introduction by the editor, which gracefully gives context to the piece and its author without unnecessarily weighing down the anthology as a whole.

The thirteen sections in this anthology are divided thematically rather than chronologically, which works well on the whole. For those that prefer a more straightforward progression of Nevada literature through the decades, there is a useful chronological list of contents in the appendix. The thematic sections roughly follow Nevada literary history. The first section records Paiute, Washoe, and Shoshone stories, such as the origin of the water babies, spirits said to live in Pyramid Lake. Section two contains excerpts from the journals of early Nevada explorers, such as John C. Fremont and George M. Wheeler. Next come writings from early emigrants traveling through what is now present-day Nevada on the Overland Trail. The dire descriptions of desert landsacpe in these selections, such as those by Virginia Reed Murphy, of the legendary Donner Party, or Sarah Royce, who rejoices once her family safely reaches the Carson River exclaiming that they "had conquered the desert," might be contrasted with the descriptions of the desert in the final section, "Wild Nevada: Lessons of the Land." Here authors such as George R. Stewart and Stephen Trimble show that with greater knowledge of the place one gains "a new way of seeing, a shifted perspective, from which the same place becomes luminous, fascinating, valuable" (723).

In the section entitled "Literary Riches from the Mining Frontier" you will find the expected humorous offerings from Mark Twain and Dan De Quille alongside an account by Mrs. Hugh Brown of what it was like for a young San Francisco bride, "trained for nothing except how to be a lady," to arrive in Tonopah in 1904 and the fascinating story of a lone mining woman, Josie Pearl, in "Queen of the Black Rock Country" written by "roving reporter of the desert," Nell Murbarger. Ranching life is given its literary exploration in "The Other Nevada: Reflections on Rural Life" as well as a separate section devoted to cowboy poetry, a genre that Elko may be given credit for revitalizing since it began the annual Cowboy Poetry Gathering in 1985. The section on Reno is full of contrasts. Walter Van Tilburg Clark calls Reno "the city of trembling leaves" (287). In the excerpt from his book of the same name, the different neighborhoods and sections of Reno are given their own character, mood, and theme as if Reno itself were a symphony. Meanwhile, Jill Stern, who came to Reno in the 1950s for a divorce and then later wrote a novel about a divorce-seeker's experience in Reno, has her character Sara think "Reno isn't a place ... It's just a symbol to America and the rest of the world; a symbol of failure to some, of release to others." Max Miller writes of the effect that the space around Reno has on the wounded psyches of those who have come there for a divorce and the healthful shock that a place like Pyramid Lake must give as they momentarily see themselves and their troubles as insignificant in time and space. The anthology also contains sections on Las Vegas, Nevada travel writing, and, interestingly, on Nevada's nuclear testing and waste concerns. The two sections that seem a bit incongruous amongst these solid themes are "Contemporary Poetry" and "Contemporary Fiction." Contemporary fiction and poetry is scattered throughout several of the other sections, however, as these selections were deemed to not quite fit with any of the other themes and were given their own space. Although this approach breaks up the neat Nevada-themed categories, it seems worth the break to be introduced to authors such as poet Gailmarie Pahmeier and fiction writer Teresa Jordan.

In this collection we see the divorce ranches of Reno and the gambling dens of Vegas set in contrast with the silence and acceptance of the desert and the seeming timelessness of Nevada's mountainous geography. Yet, as Bernard Schopen's novel, *The Big Silence*, states in its opening lines: "In Nevada, nothing is as it seems" (645). Selections such as the excerpt from John McPhee's *Basin and Range* show that the landscape is not everlasting but rather changing in fascinating ways. Meanwhile, stories such as that excerpted from William J. Plummer's *A Quail in the Family* show timeless human values, such as family bonding and care for other species set in the heart of Las Vegas. We are allowed to understand both the suffering and anguish that this land brought to Sarah Royce as she tries to get her family across the desert in a covered wagon and the fascination and curiosity, even a feeling of friendship, that it awakens in Ann Haymond Zwinger as she hikes through it nearly 150 years later. Author Jim Sloan tells us that "The only way to explain Nevada is by telling stories about it" (762). One story cannot be enough. This anthology gives us many stories told in many voices so that the complexity of the land, its people, and its history shines through. ∎

Alisha A. Sullivan
University of Nevada, Reno

Barber, Alicia. *Reno's Big Gamble: Image and Reputation in the Biggest Little City*. Lawerence, KS: University Press of Kansas, 2008. 320 pages, illus. $34.95—Reno has been so uncomfortable with is own image that, in its nearly 150 years in existence, no one has either offered or successfully delivered a full consideration of the town's history. Some historians, academics and buffs alike, have covered aspects of the city, such as its economy, its architecture, or its culture, but none have provided a full and detailed profile. In what was to be the most complete history of the city, John M. Townley promised three volumes of his history entitled *Tough Little Town on the Truckee*, but only published the first volume. This is why Alicia Barber's book, *Reno's Big Gamble: Image and Reputation in the Biggest Little City*, is such a welcome and crucial addition to the historical literature of Reno.

Barber's work, an extension of her doctoral dissertation completed at the University of Texas, combines a multi-disciplinary approach written in a sharp, historical style. Like most historians, she leans heavily on sociological, anthropological, and cultural themes as she delves into the historical perception of Reno from abroad and from within. By virtue of her study of Reno in terms of "place identity," though, her study of Reno is as much environmental literature as it is an historical text.

"Place identity," as defined in her book, is studied through the "civic reputation" of the community and location. "Civic reputation" is in turn defined as "the governing reputation of a city or town from the outside," and is constantly evolving and consists of two major components: "sense of place" and "promoted image." A "sense of place" is "often inspired by the natural environment" and is simply "the sense of being at home in a city or town." Conversely, the "promoted image" is "aspirational and idealistic, embodying how officials would best like a place to be perceived." These three components come together in the form of the place itself, a factor that is most prone to physical change and most likely to be the object of the public ire if there is extreme dissonance between "sense of place" and "promoted image." With these tools, Barber analyzes Reno as well as the conflicts between "sense of place" and "promoted image" that play out over the years (see pg. 5).

Barber's approach to the evolution of Reno's image is arranged chronologically in six, in-depth and painstakingly researched chapters. She opens with the city's founding in 1868 and continues through the turn of the 20th Century, when Reno was struggling to gain its footing as a true city and no longer merely a train stop on the way to mining destinations in Nevada and California. It was here that Reno's defining conflict first became apparent: Situated among beautiful natural environs and containing rich natural resources and an increasingly stable community, it had to confront a nation that still recognized it as a transient town with morals to match.

In the 20th Century, as Barber continues, Reno began to embrace its image as a libertarian outpost. Gambling, easy divorces, and prize fights to the finish—all activities that were frowned upon nationally, but were accepted, albeit not categorically, by a city that was eager to frame its lax legal requirements as manifestations of the city's progressive stance towards modernity. The boosters of the State and the city began to capitalize on the reputation it had cultivated. Striving for a unique "urban personality," the city seemed to recognize that real money was to be made in letting people do as they wished within a regulated environment (see pg. 85). This theme continues for the remainder of the book as Barber describes national and local changes and the marketing innovations all of which impacted the way Reno was perceived at home and abroad.

One of the most prominent themes in Barber's book is the duality of Reno's nature, and how it was embraced, rejected, and interpreted throughout the years. She cites many other scholars of many other disciplines that describe the city's "schizophrenia" (see pg. 3). This discussion is repeated in many instances throughout the book, often pitched as the residents' desire to have respectability in a city known for allowing and even encouraging vice. The struggle to define the "real Reno" against the "other Reno" would eventually settle itself in a comfortable, 21st Century, postmodern approach where residents and boosters alike grew to accept and appreciate the city for its ability constantly to transform, while maintaining the many attributes that the locals had grown to love (see pg. 250).

If there is anything for which the book might be criticized, it is likely to be the distinct difference in the author's approach to the city in the first three chapters versus the subsequent three chapters. In the opening chapters, Barber takes great pains to discuss the people, the institutions, and the specific legislative changes that resulted in tremendous impacts on the city's reputation. In the latter half of the book, Barber's analysis becomes far broader, and by necessity, far more selective in the use of evidence to support her overarching points. While this change in approach should be noted, it can easily be explained with several concessions to the author. First, the nature of the nation and the city changed tremendously, and many different elements impacted the city's reputation in the latter half of the 20th Century and the beginning of the 21st. Second, even the best special collections, and even the most of obscure of which seem to have been explored by Barber in her research for this volume, contain limited sources from long ago in Nevada's history, while the digital age has allowed for the retention of vast quantities of usable data for a researcher. And third, the difference between Barber's approach only serves to reinforce how much the city has grown, changed, and the reasons for both.

Barber's book is an exciting and tremendous addition to the body of work that chronicles Reno's history. It is perhaps the first complete approach to the city's past will serve as the academic standard for Reno's first 150 years for those who wish to understand why Reno is the way it is and why its image is such a tricky balancing act. It is no slight to other authors who have attempted to capture the essence of Reno's history in previous volumes to describe *Reno's Big Gamble* as such, but rather an indication that Reno has finally come into its own in a way that is understandable. ∎

Caleb S. Cage
The Nevada Review

Paher, Stanley W. *Nevada Ghost Towns and Mining Camps* **(Historical and Old West). Howel-North Publishing Co., 1970. 492 pages. $54.95**—In my business as a bookseller, I am often asked which book to start with in an inquiry into the history of Nevada. While notable literary authors, including Robert Laxalt and Effie Mona Mack, have written fine informative histories of Nevada, I always suggest Stanley Paher's *Nevada Ghost Towns and Mining Camps.*

I purchased my first copy of this book in 1972, and I still have my original copy. Through my many years of hunting, prospecting, and business travel around the state, I have referred back to *Nevada Ghost Towns and Mining Camps* to keep informed about the history of the places I visited. I am not alone in this reliance on Paher's work for Nevada history, as the book has gone through 14 printings with over 67,000 copies printed.

While Paher's work does not set out to be a general history of Nevada, the comprehensive coverage of the mining camp era makes it indispensable for understanding the development of Nevada as a state and the background of the formation of modern Nevada. This book differs from most histories in that it is not organized chronologically or by subject, but rather geographically. The entire book consists of short histories of the many mining towns and camps that sprang up, sometimes grew, and then declined in the last half of the nineteenth century and the first half of the 20th century. Again, these vignettes are organized geographically by county.

The idiosyncrasies of the work are the result of the approach and motivations of the author. Stanley Paher was born and raised in Las Vegas. As a young man still in his teens, he became enchanted with the Nevada desert and the numerous ghost towns scattered around the state. He would typically spend his weekends in the desert exploring the various mining sites and the remains of towns that were much more in evidence at that time. In short, he became a young "desert rat." His curiosity about the history of these areas led him to spend more and more time searching for historical records and old photographs to shed light on the origins of the towns and mines that he had visited. In the process, he accumulated an extensive library and archives of Nevada histories, photographs and ephemera. He also met and interviewed a number of the old-timers that had been involved directly in the Nevada mining booms and busts. The publication of *Nevada Ghost Towns and Mining Camps* in 1970 by Howell-North Books was the result of this very personal project of historical research.

Paher's historical vignettes paint a wonderful picture of a unique era in Western American history. All aspects of historical development are touched upon as they relate to the different towns and times. There is information on the westward migration, military activities in Nevada, the development of ranching and farming, transportation, education, religion, social life, and especially the mining and mineral milling industries. The focus on the mining camps makes this a history of the common man. The personalities are not Nevada's governors, senators, and socialites, but rather the prospectors, miners, promoters, gamblers, prostitutes, merchants, criminals, freighters, and saloon keepers striving to make a living and establish a civilization in the great Nevada desert.

The narrow focus of this book necessarily omits many facets of Nevada history that the serious student will want to pursue in other works. There are many books addressing pre-history, political history, railroad history, histories of the modern cities, and other subjects that are not extensively treated in *Nevada Ghost Towns and Mining Camps*, but there is no other book that recreates the flavor of early Nevada in the same way as this important work.

Since the book was written nearly 40 years ago, there have been many changes in the Nevada landscape, including the growth of the cities and towns, modern mining operations, and improvements in the highway system. Therefore, much of the contemporary information in the book describing existing conditions and directions to the locations has become obsolete. In order to remedy this, the author has created the *Nevada Ghost Towns and Desert Atlas*. The *Atlas* has sold over 30,000 copies and is now in its 7th printing. The new edition contains 71 up-to-date color maps showing the locations of the ghost towns described in *Nevada Ghost Towns and Mining Camps* as well as many recreational areas in Nevada and Death Valley.

In the 1970s, one of the common sights around Reno was an old green Jeep Wagoneer driven by Stan Paher with signs emblazoned on both sides that read "READ NEVADA GHOST TOWNS AND MINING CAMPS." If you have any interest in Nevada history, that advice is just as good today as it was then. ∎

Lee Johnson
Zephyr Books, Reno, Nevada

Made in the USA
Charleston, SC
21 November 2009